What I Want to Talk About

of related interest

Bittersweet on the Autism Spectrum
Edited by Luke Beardon, PhD and Dean Worton
ISBN 978 1 78592 207 7
eISBN 978 1 78450 485 4

An Adult with an Autism Diagnosis
A Guide for the Newly Diagnosed
Gillan Drew
ISBN 978 1 78592 246 6
eISBN 978 1 78450 530 1

Living in Two Worlds
On Being a Social Chameleon with Asperger's
Dylan Emmons
ISBN 978 1 78592 706 5
eISBN 978 1 78450 263 8

Sex, Drugs and Asperger's Syndrome (ASD)
A User Guide to Adulthood
Luke Jackson
Foreword by Tony Attwood
ISBN 978 1 84905 645 8
eISBN 978 1 78450 139 6

Pretending to be Normal
Living with Asperger's Syndrome (Autism
Spectrum Disorder) Expanded Edition
Liane Holliday Willey
ISBN 978 1 84905 755 4
eISBN 978 0 85700 987 6

What I Want to Talk About

HOW AUTISTIC SPECIAL INTERESTS SHAPE A LIFE

Pete Wharmby

Jessica Kingsley Publishers
London and Philadelphia

First published in Great Britain in 2023 by Jessica Kingsley Publishers
An imprint of Hodder & Stoughton Ltd
An Hachette Company

1

Front cover image source: Kara McHale.

A CIP catalogue record for this title is available from
the British Library and the Library of Congress

ISBN 978 1 78775 827 8
eISBN 978 1 78775 828 5

Printed and bound in Great Britain by Clays Limited

Jessica Kingsley Publishers' policy is to use papers that are natural,
renewable and recyclable products and made from wood grown in
sustainable forests. The logging and manufacturing processes are expected
to conform to the environmental regulations of the country of origin.

Jessica Kingsley Publishers
Carmelite House
50 Victoria Embankment
London EC4Y 0DZ

www.jkp.com

For my grandad,
who always listened.

Contents

Introduction

Hyperfixations and monotropism

This book is not a memoir. There are two significant reasons for this. One is that my life to date does not warrant a memoir – I have experienced far too few exciting things in my almost 40 years to fill the pages of a traditional autobiography. The other is that I hope many exciting things may still be to come, in which case there is a chance I will be writing my memoir, let us just say... some other time. No; this is no stately jaunt carefully picking through the years since my birth to the present day. It is not a character study of how I went from being a tiny, slightly grumpy baby to the huge, slightly grumpy man I am today; nor will it give insight into the challenges of my life, the paths not taken, the successes, the boredom.

Instead, this is a book that is about probably the most important things to me – the things that, as far as I'm concerned, make me *me*, and also make me autistic, and also make me interesting, at least some of the time. This is a book about the things that keep me going in life; the things that focus my energy, that keep me afloat, that calm me in times of stress, that thrill me in times of peace; the things that grasp and hold my attention like a dangled length of string occupies a kitten; it is a book about my interests.

Special Interests, we tend to call them. All autistic people have them to some extent. If you are reading this as an autistic person, you will know precisely what I mean. If you are not, then hold up – let's take a moment to understand them. Special Interests (I capitalize them to bestow the adequate amount of importance to the words) are rather like what you may call 'hobbies' or 'pastimes'. When I say, 'rather like', I am afraid I'm straining the simile to breaking point as, although it is a helpful comparison, it doesn't come close to doing the phenomenon of Special Interests justice. A hobby is something you do to while away the time between *a* and *b*, an enjoyable and usually productive endeavour that marks the significant difference between work and play. All people have hobbies, or at least the capacity for them. They are universal.

Special Interests (or Hyperfixations, as I tend to call them) are not universal. They are the domain of the neurotype subset we refer to as autistic people, and to a certain extent those with ADHD. They are much more than hobbies. More powerful, more potent, more intense, more important. It is unlikely that a non-autistic person would be able to sufficiently imagine exactly how this feels, but I will try to help you do just that. A Hyperfixation is an interest in a topic, idea, thing or things that shares two key traits. One is that the interest is intrusive, cropping up regularly in your thoughts whilst in the middle of other things, often to the point of having to drop everything to indulge in it, and the second is that it is inexhaustible – an autistic person's interest in a Hyperfixation will never tire or dwindle. As you will see as you read, the interests I describe here have mostly been with me for years and years – often since early childhood – and I am yet to truly tire of any of them.

So, to give a slightly stereotypical example, an autistic person may have a Special Interest in trains. A common enough phenomenon. They may love reading about trains, playing with train models, designing trains and track lay-outs, reading timetables, studying maps of tracks and so on and so forth. So far, so hobby-like. The difference is that this interest will always be there, either front and centre when being indulged, or hiding in the wings, muttering darkly about being ignored and constantly bursting onto the stage at inopportune moments, all of its own accord. I have been sitting in a meeting at work when this occurs – I find my mind wandering as I begin to doodle various locomotives from history. Then I add the Forth Rail Bridge to put them on. Then some details of cabs and funnels and whatever comes to mind. A large portion of my brain, which refuses to be distracted by mere *work*, begins to fixate on all the information I have realized I am lacking, and how I will put this right using Google the moment this damn silly meeting is over. It takes an act of real will to force a Hyperfixation back into its place in the wings, back into a place where it can once again grumble and snipe while I get on with whatever it is I need to be doing.

And when this might be, for example, feeding my daughter, or catching a bus successfully, or not stepping, distracted and vague, in front of traffic – well, that's when things can get rather difficult. One very useful word that has been increasingly used to describe the autistic frame of mind when it comes to these interests is 'monotropism' – based on the Greek for 'single attraction' or 'sole focus' – which accurately presents the reality of what seems to be going on inside my autistic brain when my interests are at the front and centre of everything that I am doing. There is a singularity of purpose that cannot be quickly swept away by external stimuli, and a single train of thought, route of focus, that cannot be deviated from and will remain in place until, for whatever reason, it is taken over by other events.

So, once my attention is captivated by whatever interest is in vogue in my psyche, my brain seems to morph from being reasonably pliable and bendy, able to change topic and move attention around with some ease (though not as much as a neurotypical person may experience), to being a one-track line with no passing spaces, no laybys, sidings or exits, no way to deviate. I become monotropic. My attention is entirely focused on the one thing, like an expensive computer that is capable of all sorts of exciting things using all of its processing power to mine a crypto-currency. In this state, the world passes me by. If I allow myself to, I can go on in this frame of mind for hours and hours and hours, with the only thing likely to drag me out of it being my ever-conflicting probable ADHD, which – in opposition to pretty much all of my autistic traits – will eventually start shouting, 'Say, what is this shit, I want to do all the other things, right now.'

Until that happens, though, I can forget to have a glass of water or cup of tea and realize much later I have a terrible headache from the dehydration. I can realize I have missed appointments, meetings, important stuff that I really could not afford to miss. I can forget to eat, ending up weak with a need for some kind of calorific intake after six or seven hours working on the same project. I can forget to go to use the toilet. I can forget to go to bed. Monotropism can be a tricky, almost dangerous trait to experience.

But it comes with huge benefits too. It is a startlingly common idea that is shared by huge numbers of neurotypical people that autistic people all have some kind of magical, inexplicable super-skill that somehow defines them as an individual. Dustin Hoffman's *Rainman* had his card counting. Stephen Wiltshire has his cities drawn from memory. However, skills of this kind are the exception, rather than the norm – autistic people *can* have amazing abilities, but then so can everyone else. Plenty of autistic people can, in fact, feel slightly sad when this topic comes up, as well-meaning folk probe with questions like 'So, you're autistic – what's your superpower?'

'Ummm, well, I can remember the music to all the levels of *Sonic the Hedgehog*?'

You can imagine how great this feels, when you know they are wondering whether you have memorized every single capital city in the world, or you can calculate planetary movement over breakfast on a bit of scrap paper, or you can tell people what day the 16th of June will be in the year 2067 without checking online.

But there is something at the heart of this stereotype. Perhaps it is not so much that we have superpowers, but more that we very frequently have topics that we simply know a great deal about, and all sorts of esoteric and specific information can emit from us, seemingly from nowhere. To an untrained, inattentive ear, this may sound very much like some kind of savant-like ability, when all it really represents is many, many hours of patient, focused study. This is what monotropism really gives us, a lot of the time: the focus to be able to absorb information on a particular topic for a great deal longer than most neurotypical people would be able to stand. This might be either active – i.e., the interest involves simply reading up on a subject, purposefully increasing your knowledge; or passive – for example, it may be that in the course of an interest you accidentally end up learning an awful lot of information about something involved with that interest, like the fact I accidentally know a lot about cars thanks to playing too many racing video games. Either way, we can seem to have vast specific reservoirs of knowledge that can appear to be quite unusual, so perhaps the savant myth perseveres thanks to this.

I have certainly managed to build up a decent reserve of general knowledge over the years. And so, Hyperfixation brings its positives and its negatives to the table. But it would be remiss of me to ignore just how much further these positives can go. Up until now I have focused heavily on monotropic interests that lend themselves to an awful lot of reading, research and knowledge retention. This is not the whole story. Hyperfixations can also be upon skills, in which case the energy and time spent is on prac-tising that skill. As we all know, hours spent on practising a skill can lead to mastery, and if our attention is entirely focused on practice, as it so often is when we trundle down the monotropic track, mastery can be achieved at a more rapid pace.

Certainly, many autistic people have skills they excel in, not through some magical genetic lottery, but through the simple application of hours upon hours of dedicated, intensely focused practice. However, when it comes to the skills themselves, the stereotypes do not hold up to the reality. Whilst the media would have it that autistic people's specialisms lie in the world of databanks and spreadsheets, physics and advanced mathematics, in actual fact what we see are a vast range of skills across the whole gamut of abilities, from cooking to dancing, comedy writing to car maintenance. There appears to be no limit to the nature of the skills we can apply our monotropic minds to.

Special Interests, our ability to hyperfocus and become monotropic, lie behind these successes and, whatever difficulties being autistic can throw at us (and there are a lot), these interests can make us specialists, experts even, in a wide variety of fields *and* tremendously skilled artists, writers, musicians, comedians and designers. Even though we might struggle to cope with the day-to-day challenges of simply existing in a neurotypical world, we still have these skills and knowledge sets to help us through, per-haps even to make our living from. In short, they are not to be sneezed at.

Our lives are a struggle though, so much of the time. It is possible in my positivity about Hyperfixations that I have glossed over the difficulties a little. I do that sometimes, as do many autistic folk, as we are trained from a young age to try to accept our struggles without complaint and push through them alone and without support. It is hard to break through that kind of conditioning; so, I will say it again, in order to remind myself as much as you of the reality: our lives are a struggle. We live with our different brain architecture in a world not designed for us, nor by us. Our experience of the world does not synchronize with your neurotypical experience, and communication between us can be difficult, not so much as if we are speaking different languages but more that we are speaking different existences, way beyond just the world of words, if we are speaking verbally at all.

Whilst many autistic people can learn to camouflage themselves to fit into this world, many cannot, and anyway, such masking of the truth is expensive in terms of energy and wellbeing. It is difficult, and the second, perhaps more important, aspect of Special Interests is how soothing and comforting they are for us, how they are always there for us and allow us a safe space to de-stress and relax (though I am still convinced the concept of 'relaxation' is a myth used to motivate ADHD people to eat their breakfast and brush their hair). It is in our Special Interests and time spent in a monotropic frame of mind where we can be ourselves without having to worry about looking or acting odd and getting mocked for our voices, gaits or eccentricities. In some cases, our interests are the closest we get to friends;

in other cases, they are the closest we get to holidays. In still more, they are the closest we get to peace.

It is this aspect of autistic Special Interests that I really want to celebrate with this book. Sure, I will talk a lot about how my Hyperfixations have led to knowledge and understanding of the world, but more I want to show you how they made my life what it is, how they helped me, guided me, gave me energy, hope and focus.

But there is one other purpose behind this book, and it is given away by its title. Ever since I was a child, I desperately wanted others to be as interested in my interests as I was. Every time I brought them up in conversation, I hoped the other person would be intrigued and engage. It hardly ever happened, and it hardly ever happens to other autistic children and adults either. We so often go through life believing no one cares enough about what we really want to talk about. Well, perhaps you will take something away from this book. Perhaps you will enjoy, *finally*, hearing about the things I love. And perhaps it will encourage you to share the things you love too or listen to other autistic people's words. If you go away from this book having learned a little about LEGO®, about Warhammer, about the *Titanic*, Marvel films and *Minecraft*®, then perhaps I can rest easy a little, after all these years.

This book isn't a memoir. It is a love letter to the phenomenon of autistic Hyperfixation. I hope you enjoy it.

Disclaimer

I want to clarify that though I will talk in general terms

about autism throughout this book, autism is not mono-lithic and has an enormously wide variety of presenta-tions. What may be true for one autistic person may not be true for another. I am basing the majority of my com-ments on a combination of my own personal experience with being autistic and my experience of sharing with the wider autistic community. Wherever possible I will highlight that these experiences may vary from person to person, and a good rule of thumb is to remember that though there is some commonality of experience with autism, you will *always* find at least one person who does not fit that description, and that is genuinely something to cherish.

CHAPTER ONE

Self, Identity, Diagnosis and LEGO®

Growing up, I readily acknowledged that I did not function like the other children I shared classrooms, playgrounds, and time with; looking back, I think I was quite proud of this fact. There is something about being different that produces a harsh and paradoxical dichotomy: on the one hand, you feel alone, isolated, targeted; on the other you feel aloof, separate, interesting. All of these latter terms are, of course, simply more positive synonyms of the former but that's the nature of it, as you live the life of an outcast simultaneously with the life of an eccentric, depending more or less on the whims of the people around you. One early episode that nicely illustrates this was when I was in Year Three at primary school. I was new to the place, having moved to the old mining town of Coalville from Loughborough (I grew up all over North Leicestershire, in the heart of England) over the Easter holidays, and was finding my feet in the class of the slightly intense Mrs Marshfield. Inevitably, I'd committed some social faux pas at the end of the day: an act of sheer, smiling ignorance that I can't recall the exact nature of, and one of the other kids turned to me and in their unequivocal Coalville way spat, 'You *wanker*.'

Bear in mind we were only eight years old. I'd heard the word and associated it vaguely with adulthood and maturity – I guess I knew it was a *naughty* word, but I had zero idea of its meaning or even its implication. I responded with a genuine grin and an earnest 'thanks!' that left the other boy confused and mentally striking my name and face from his list of people it was ok to sit next to in assembly. This was not an act of bravado or even bravery: it was an act of sheer naivety. At the time I had no insight into what had happened – when you are eight years old, things just *happen*. However, nowadays I can look back at this and recognize it for what it was: a fundamental misreading of social cues.

I had assumed, in the absence of any evidence that I had done anything wrong, that this peer of mine was ribbing me in that particularly masculine way (we would now call it *banter*, I suppose) that young boys with certain types of fathers have. You see, I had come across that phenomenon before and made a note of it. This is something that autistic children have to do: months and months of communicative baby-steps leading, inevitably but exhaustingly, to a kind of mental almanac of reference points that can be used to carefully guide the individual through the alarmingly unforgiving minefield of social interaction. My almanac was growing steadily. I observed everything and took note of everything – subconsciously of course – so that I may never feel again the sting of miscommunication, the pain of getting the wrong end of the stick. So, I had resorted to a recent entry to my internal reference book, marked 'sarcastic praise', and identified it as so. Thus, I grinned. I was part of the group, accepted by a child of the same age as me.

But, of course, it had been an insult.

I realized this around 30 seconds later when half the class were looking at me and stifling laughter (they had to stifle it – our teacher may have missed me being accused of overzealous masturbation, but they were certainly not going to let any childlike jollity go unpunished). My internal systems, like a man who's been shot but hasn't realized it yet, continued with the charade of expecting they were laughing *with* me – a kind of friendly laughter of solidarity – but reality dawned quickly, and I felt the metaphorical bullet in the ribs. They were laughing *at* me. Once again, for a reason I was unable to identify, let alone rectify, I was a figure of fun and mockery to the other children in the class. I added 'wanker' into my databank of 'things it is not pleasant to be called' and got on with my day. Thirty years later and I still think about it from time to time.

The thing is, developing this almanac of social cues and understanding takes a great deal of effort. You spend an awful lot of time updating it during a time when any other child – any other neurotypical child, that is – would be busy growing a personality. As an autistic person, I had no time for this. I did not grow a personality: I built one. It is a common thing to hear from autistic adults, that they feel they are not entirely sure who they really are. Autistic people, in their endless updating of their social behaviour almanac, often take snippets and excerpts of other people's personalities and graft them together into an ill-fitting mask that then passes as their external personality. We update our social databanks with Person A's self-deprecating humour, for example, or Person B's easy-going attitude; I saw what worked for others and naturally incorporated these things into my own personality (hard hats required, under construction) so that I too may experience the easy social interactions that everyone else seemed to enjoy. Over time this long, tiring, yet staggeringly creative process begins to eradicate the horribly uncomfortable 'You wanker' moments – piece by piece, brick by brick, a personality is formed that has one express goal: to avoid humiliation, shame, embarrassment.

For that is what drove me. I was desperate to be liked, to be accepted, not necessarily to be loved, but certainly regarded with fondness. I was (and remain) terrified of people thinking badly of me, or criticism of any kind (I will be avoiding all reviews of this book, for example), and the thought of conflict – particularly conflict instigated by myself – is abhorrent to me. A childhood of miserably messing up every single social interaction will do this to a person. So, my mask was built, slowly but inevitably, as I soaked up social experiences, setbacks, nightmares and successes. The next time someone called me a wanker (and it took a surprisingly long time to happen), I had learned the scripts, honed the mask, made ready with the appropriate response to ensure I would never look so foolish as I did in Mrs Marshfield's class so long ago: I looked the man straight in the eye, smiled knowingly and said with a self-deprecating shake of the head, learned probably from Harrison Ford or Bill Murray, 'Yeah, I know, I just can't help myself.' The situation was immediately defused, the danger had passed, the pub went back to being a place of conviviality rather than confrontation. My almanac, and its long, painful investment, had paid off.

✤

As I constructed a personality, free of the helpful benefits of having a diagnosis of autism, I also took a great interest in the way everything else around me was constructed too. I couldn't say if there was a conscious link, but a fascination with buildings and their designs has always been a part of my life. This love of architecture was fostered by my father who, I would later learn, almost certainly shared my very specific manifestation of autism. My father's idea of a fun weekend trip with a toddler in tow usually involved, at least in part, time spent near to (or often *in*) a building without a roof, windows or floors – one of the many ruined old stately homes or manors that dot the Midlands. A favourite of my father was the hulking, extraordinarily dark and brooding remains of Sutton Scarsdale Hall just off the M1 in Derbyshire – a place whose name seems tremendously fitting for such a place, as if it were named such in anticipation of it eventually becoming a dark and brooding ruin – where we would wander around, my mother usually following in vague bemusement, spotting the places in the walls where floor joists and such would have once been inserted into walls.

Moments of indescribable joy for both father and son occurred whenever we spotted original interior elements such as decorated alcoves, fireplace surrounds or architraving: anything that provided proof that this desiccated shell of a building was once a comfortable home. Many happy summer hours were spent in such places – Trentham Gardens near Stoke on Trent, Garendon Park on the outskirts of Loughborough, Witley Court in Worcestershire – analysing how the past slotted in to the strangely unsatisfying present landscape, before decamping to a nearby pub for the inevitable pint of ale my father would need after a morning of such social exuberance (a habit I would pick up, and one that I'm sure many autistic readers will identify with). I would have a bottle of Panda cola and a bag of those intense scampi fries that were ubiquitous in the 80s and 90s. I can't for the life of me recall what my mother had – my attention on these day trips into the past was firmly on both my dad and the places we saw, but I would hazard a guess at a gin and tonic and a scowl – she had to (still has to, being probably the only non-autistic person in the family) put up with an awful lot, my poor mum.

Our shared obsession, I think, was with permanence. We were uninterested in what had changed in both the ruined houses and the landscape, and far more focused on what had managed, against all odds, to remain. The joy of finding some surviving stuccoed plasterwork was based on the surprise that it had made it to the present, against the threats of fire, wind, rain, vandalism – almost as if it had sustained itself by sheer will. My father and I lived for spotting these tiny, brave details and we discussed them gravely, at length, on the drive back home. Living in Loughborough, we were right by the grounds of what once was Garendon Hall – an impressive stately pile that had been demolished in the 1960s but had once belonged to the prominent De Lisle family of North Leicestershire. The grounds were extensive and had various little architectural treats dotted around them. I knew the word 'obelisk', I would say, long before any of my contemporaries at Booth Wood Primary School, thanks to the huge one that scratched the sky as it rose above the dark woods at the eastern end of the grounds, and the Triumphal Arch and Temple of Venus were such key landmarks that to this day I can easily see them in my head whenever I fancy mentally revisiting them, and eagerly look out for them whenever I visit Loughborough to see my university friends who have ended up teaching where they learned.

Ruins are so much more interesting than healthy, happy buildings. They have so much more to say, so much more to share with you if you take the time to look at them carefully. I had an unfortunate habit of enjoying breaking toys, in order to experience the decay I'd seen first-hand. I remember being given some Airfix models – those sets you glue together and paint in a vain attempt to create something like the image on the box – that had been finished by some unknown hand. In my memory they were brilliantly detailed ships, and must have been a metre long, though I doubt they actually were. My first instinct, and thus my first action, was to take a bath with them and give them what could be described as the 'Pearl

Harbor' treatment. I studied the mangled wrecks of these poor boats so carefully over the next few days, looking for what had survived – what had managed to weather the terrible onslaught I'd inflicted upon them in a bubble bath, oblivious to the fact I had totally ruined them forever. It is no wonder my parents introduced me to a toy that could allow me to explore these destructive needs.

LEGO®.

It is fitting that the first proper Hyperfixation that I tell you about is LEGO®, given that out of all the things I have found my brain taking solace in over the course of my life, it is the sole genuine constant. Ever since I received my first bricks, it has never strayed far from my thoughts for any amount of time – I promise that by the time you have finished this book you will realize I intend no hyperbole here whatsoever.

My first LEGO® was, as I'm sure is common for a lot of children given its price, a hand-me-down from my older cousins who lived on a quiet 1970s cul-de-sac nearby. It was quintessential early 1980s LEGO®, already quite aged by the time I got my eager hands all over it, and I wondered then whether they had been freely parted from it. Having said that, both of my teenage cousins were, as far as I was concerned, far more fully functioning as human males than I was as an already self-consciously awkward six-year-old, so I'm sure they didn't mourn the passage of their toys to their young cousin as much as I would have done. It was a mixture of the 'classic' Space LEGO® sets, all grey and blue with transparent yellow windows that is so truly beloved today (the character Benny from

The LEGO® Movie is based on this era of spaceship-loving sets) and yellow architectural pieces – all archways and windows that, predictably enough, my father took more of an interest in.

And so, architecture and LEGO® came together as my father and I spent time constructing the mansion ruins we had explored in person. It was always the same. My father would put some Albinoni on the CD player and settle to build the footprint of our latest project – always two courses of red brick as a foundation followed by the rest in yellow – carefully placing the window and doorway openings in order to recreate the majesty of the imposing buildings we'd explored. Meanwhile, I would be faffing around with the other pieces, making disagreeable little vehicles and animals that I hoped I would have an opportunity to ram violently against the walls of my dad's big house once he had finished. In my memory, he never did finish a house, though I am sure I'm wrong about that. I do know they were never roofed. I think he pretended even to himself he was reconstructing the houses in their original glory, when really he was just building more fascinating ruins.

Following these escapades, proper boxed LEGO® sets were the natural progression – bricks that you used to build the design on the front of the box. Contrary to what a lot of people seem to believe, LEGO® has released sets with instructions for decades, and they also continue to market boxes of miscellaneous bricks: for some reason the company gets a lot of casual criticism for abandoning randomness in favour of planned sets as if it were a recent, millennial travesty rather than a cornerstone of their business model since the 1950s.

My first set I remember opening was a Shell garage, back when LEGO® still did commercial sponsorships with oil companies – such a thing would be absolute public relations kryptonite these days – and the set featured the logo fairly prominently, in a bold move to advertise petrochemicals to the under-sevens. Despite this naked profiteering, I found these sets opened up a whole new world for me: the ability to craft narratives. They were a storyteller's dream! I could have my principal protagonists go to the local pizzeria where they'd sit under the majestic, curved glass windows, before hopping in their strangely cramped yellow city car off to the petrol station, where an inevitable shoot-out would occur leading to the terrifying destruction of the entire town, possibly with the intervention of aliens, with the harbour police finding their reasons to get involved despite most of the action taking place inland. I could construct storylines for hours upon hours with these bricks, relishing the ability to have terrible chaos that could be fixed and reverted to normal after 30 minutes of careful rebuilding. For a child with a vivid imagination and an obsession with destruction and ruin, this was the toy. It was the only toy I would ever really need.

My favourite phase of a bout of super-devastation on the bedroom floor was the period of quiet reflection that took place after the action had wound down and the smoke cleared. Like my trips with my mum and dad to view what remained of real ruins, I would gaze at the remains of the buildings, cars, trucks with reverence, enjoying the revelation that somehow the fire station's control tower was still standing, though at a haphazard angle. I'd wander around the scene with my eyes, as I had done with my parents around the ruins of Regency England, absorbing the spectacle of annihilation, emulating the quiet hissing and tocking sounds of burned-out vehicles, utterly and superbly engrossed. It is interesting to me now, 30 years later, how fascinated I have always been with the inevitability of entropy, as my own life begins to splinter at the seams from being autistic for too long in a hostile world.

Looking back, I think LEGO® afforded me a way to vent off my frustrations without finding myself in too much trouble. Smashing a police station to pieces with a fire truck was preferable to vandalizing school property, for example, or developing a violent stim of some kind. In fact, LEGO® became a stim all of its own. 'Stimming' is the informal name given to an action, sound or movement that acts as a mood stabilizer for autistic people. Everyone has the capacity to stim – the classic tropes of pacing back and forth when worried or tapping your fingers when impatient stem from the same impulse – yet it is autistic people who have stimming as a very important and intense part of their daily life, mostly because those extremes of emotion that trigger this behaviour in non-autistics are pretty much a daily occurrence for autistic people.

Some folks stim by moving a part of their body, by rocking, by clenching their toes – I ended up stimming through fiddling with LEGO® bricks. The bricks themselves are an absolute marvel of engineering. People go on about how impressive dams and skyscrapers are, when in reality the most awesome design is the humble two by four stud LEGO® brick. They are designed so meticulously, so minutely that they will continue to clip together tightly (not so tightly that you cannot separate them, and not loose enough to fall apart) after thousands and thousands of repeated uses. They are, to all intents and purposes, indestructible – try snapping a standard brick – and bricks from 70 years ago still fit together with brand new ones fresh from the factory. As such, the sensation when you push two bricks together is simply sublime, and is one of my very favourite things in the world. I would take a pocketful of LEGO® to school every morning, using it to help regulate my stress levels – if I was feeling pressured or confused at school (and this happened far more than my teachers would have been aware) I would surreptitiously take two bricks and clip them together, break them apart, clip, break, clip, break, enjoying their solid, satisfying feeling. Other autistic children may have fidgeted or called out: I simply sat quietly eroding plastic bricks with my fingers. I still do this. These days, my school teaching days behind me, I do a lot of online tutoring. In my hands you will always find a few LEGO® bricks that I can quietly squeeze together and pry apart.

But what about the attractiveness of the toy? I remember telling the psychiatrist who diagnosed me with autism in 2017 that I saw LEGO® as 'jewels' or 'gems': highly coloured, shiny, precious objects through which I just wanted to run my fingers, or better bathe in, like Scrooge McDuck and his gold coins. I am certain this was the point of my diagnostic interview at which the doctor finally ticked the box marked 'hell yes, they're autistic'. I feel the sensory joy of LEGO® is by no means limited to the feel of them connecting. The small transparent round plates are the best – the ones you may have used as car headlights in your youth. They shine in a vast variety of colours and, being see through, glint gaudily in the light from any angle. They may be plastic, but to my mind they are not far removed from diamonds and emeralds. Having piles of them to pick from when building a set is a sensory joy that is hard to beat. Some people, when they open a new set, spend a happy few hours separating the bricks up into colours, creating neat little piles of colour-coded satisfaction before the building work even begins and, as an autistic person, I salute this dedication to the art of organization and sorting. But my heart belongs to the chaos and work involved in scraping through a huge pile of plastic rubies, emeralds, sapphires, opals and garnets to find the elusive piece I need; doing otherwise feels like cheating somehow.

Apart from this, why is LEGO® such an attractive prospect for autistic people? I know that I am not alone in this, and that LEGO® features somewhere just below trains and comic books in the stereotypical list of autistic interests. In the end for me, the attraction of LEGO® is its forgiving nature. As a natural creative I adore spending time making things, but I am petrified of failing or making mistakes. Using glue, paint, or papier-mâché is a risky undertaking for someone who is liable to give up a project if something goes so wrong that the only recourse is to start over. I do not do 'starting over'. It is a total anathema to me, and I view people who will do so with a smile in their heart and a spring in their step with extreme suspicion. No, having to waste time starting from scratch is something my autistic brain cannot handle, perhaps due to my almost certain sprinkling of ADHD, which makes every second of every day precious to the point of paranoia. LEGO® does not require such horrors. Nothing is permanent in LEGO®-land. All designs can be tweaked quickly and easily with nothing more than your imagination and your fingers. No complicated or fussy cutting out or gluing or painting of individual pieces is required and for someone who thrives on a wilful lack of preparation time this is a godsend. The idea of succumbing to the admittedly tempting pleasures of loo roll tubes, sticky-backed plastic and acrylic paint was far too distasteful, too messy, too incoherent and lacking in structure. Building a replica of Tracy Island from *Thunderbirds* out of cardboard and tissue paper like they did on *Blue Peter* was no good to me as it had no clear instructions, and no scope for a rebuild if I fancied setting things up different.

LEGO® was, therefore, the toy for me.

Order and clarity are vital for many autistic people, and I am no exception. We live in a tumultuous world of constant stress, you see: a whirlpool of chaos that I doubt many neurotypical people could imagine, much less withstand. Our senses, much like those of Spider-Man, are 'dialled up to eleven' meaning we experience a brighter, more colourful, noisier, smellier, rougher, smoother, hotter, colder reality than the rest of our fellow humans, who tend to live in happy ignorance of this fact. Being assaulted by our senses is a way of life for autistics and though it can bring some positives (I pride myself on my ability to discern visual details, for example), it usually acts as a catalyst for intense stress and discomfort, meaning that autistic people take shelter in anything that reduces this weight of stress.

Order, routine, logic – these are safe harbours in the terrible storm and many of us, even the most creative and independent, need these to stay mentally healthy. To help any neurotypical people reading this, no doubt open-mouthed at the horrors I am describing, imagine those times you had to turn the radio down in the car when irritably trying to find somewhere to park outside your destination – why did you do this? Much humour can be derived from the seeming pointlessness of such an action (reminding me of the beautifully redundant line 'Listen, can you smell something?' from famously autistic actor Dan Aykroyd in *Ghostbusters*) yet it is actually rooted in sense. When your brain is engaged with something complex – in this case trying to spot a house number from 20 metres (why do they make the numerals so small?) – any extra input is undesirable and can, quite frankly, sod off. You turn the radio off as it is distracting you and filling your brain with nonsense when you need it nice and empty for the task at hand. And it is worse the louder the music, yes? If someone in their haste to turn the radio off on your barked command accidentally turned it *up*, I think we all know what the outcome would be. Someone is walking home.

Well, for an autistic person it is like there is always a

radio blaring noisily during everything we do. The sensory input that the world generally provides is the radio, and our very life is the equivalent of 'trying to find a parking space outside number 24'. Now, one way of 'turning the radio down' in our lives is to structure them in an ordered, routine way, where we do not have to deal with the stress of 'finding parking' as we already know exactly where it is and how to get to it – we have done it before a million times. This is one reason we crave routine. The way that LEGO® behaves precisely as you expect to, in its uniform and stable way, makes it ideal for those of us who crave order and familiarity as a way to help us get through the day. The addition of clear, numbered instructions explaining exactly how to go from a pile of random plastic to a rally car or medieval castle is just the icing on the orderly cake.

You see, as I alluded to at the start of this chapter, I grew up without this instruction book. I had no innate sense of how social relationships worked as I had not been shipped with this knowledge pre-installed. Instead, I had to spend my formative years frantically figuring it all out. My diagnosis of Asperger's in 2017, at the age of 34, finally provided me with the instruction booklet I needed: I was finally able to make sense of the random bricks of my personality and life and begin the process of building it in a way that actually, at long last, *worked*. I'm not saying that an autistic personality is somehow preordained – more that you have far more chance of making sense of it if you are furnished with all of the relevant details beforehand.

Being given the diagnosis, at 12.30pm in a cold afternoon

in November, by a kindly lady who had expertly guided me through the lengthy procedure, was a moment of clarity, where I felt a similar rush to when I first start a new LEGO® set and place the first pieces carefully as per the instructions. The diagnosis interviews had been long, and by this point I was fed up with the concept of neurodiversity. I had raised my suspicions that I was autistic with my doctor in the summer, and they had referred me quickly to the Wiltshire diagnostic team in Devizes, but that was the speediest section of the journey. What followed were three interminable interviews where a psychiatrist questioned me in minute detail about every single aspect of my disarmingly boring life. I believe by the end of it she knew more about my best friends at primary school than even they did.

It was all to sift through the sand and grit of my life for the shining nuggets of solid gold autism that were undoubtedly haunting Wharmby Creek, as it were. As she prospected in this manner, I felt increasingly certain I was a charlatan: that I was making it all up just to try and achieve some heinous goal that even I wasn't aware of. This form of imposter syndrome is common in many autistic people as we are trained throughout life never to make a fuss, not to rock the boat, so when we are indeed rocking the boat like a happy dog on a surfboard, we feel a distinct sense of unease and guilt. I was getting this in spades in the quiet, beige and whispering room at Devizes hospital.

The idea of being in some way different – in a way that would miraculously explain some of my most abject disappointments in life – seemed like cheating. In the same way as winning a game of monopoly by sneaking £100 out of the bank every now and again is a hollow, empty victory, getting a diagnosis of autism would be a scam committed on myself, an excuse, a way for me to pass off all my foibles and take no responsibility. I felt this keenly (still do, to a certain extent – especially when my diagnosis is questioned) and was desperate to feel sure that this psychiatrist would see past my bullshit and second guessing and make the right call. That is the thing: I was so convinced that this was just another excuse-finding exercise that I feel if I had not been impressed by the doctor's manner and professionalism, I would likely have ignored the findings in an act of such stubborn self-sabotage that it would make Walter White blush in embarrassment.

Luckily for me, and to an extent my family and friends, the doctor was excellent; she was methodical to the point of perfectionism and seemed to be piecing my psyche together out of plastic bricks herself, which warmed me to her. By the time the paperwork had come through confirming I was indeed autistic, I was content that I had not just committed an excellent wheeze to absolve myself of responsibility: rather I had finally gotten a hold on the instruction booklet for LEGO® Creator Expert set Peter Wharmby, 1983 pieces, ages 0–34.

Now it was time to make sense of myself.

✥

It was at this time that I completely outed myself as autistic to both my little world of family, friends and work, and to the wider community through means such as Twitter and my blog. It did not occur to me not to do this. After all, it was a life-changing realization and explained so many of my issues: why would I keep it to myself? Naive and blasé to the last, I opened up completely, in the process fatally wounding my career as a head of department and teacher. In being too brutally honest and open about my new limitations (I had to limit myself now if I wanted to stay mentally healthy and well), I accidentally portrayed myself as incapable of fulfilling my role and over a period of years found myself sliding first out of favour with my employers and second out of teaching itself at an accelerated rate.

I stepped down from my leadership role first: I mistakenly believed my diagnosis was not conducive to success in this field, and my resignation was accepted immediately. A few years later, battered and bruised by this self-inflicted attack on my own competence, the advent of a fatal pandemic and an increased belief I wanted to spend my time writing, I left teaching for good. It is for this reason that even in a chapter on the positivity of embracing an autistic identity, I wish to ring quiet alarm bells about my being far too green at this point and being far too open from day one. The world is not yet ready for such total honesty about neurodiversity, and whether they intend to or not, others will treat you differently after you explain that you are disabled in this manner. Disclosing your autism diagnosis is a personal decision that has to be made carefully and deliberately, with a clear understanding of what the pitfalls could potentially be.

But away from this traumatic experience, the few years since finding out my neurotype have been happier, more settled ones. It is quite something to have to rebuild your own understanding of yourself in your mid-thirties – rather like undergoing a nuclear-powered version of a mid-life crisis – and discovering how you have spent years and years actively working against your own best interests by trying too hard to fit in, too hard to be quiet and too hard to be that worst of all things: normal. These days I allow myself my limitations and avoid forcing myself to do things that I know will cause me harm down the line. Gone are the days of quietly and bitterly acquiescing to an activity that will cause years-long trauma, simply out of social embarrassment. If someone wants to do something I cannot handle now, I say so. Well, I may not be quite that clear, but I certainly refuse and run away screaming, which has the same effect. I allow myself my tics and repetitive behaviours now, without questioning myself or attacking my own psyche for being too weird for my own good. I let myself stim when I need to, and I have reduced the amount of time I spend worrying about seeming strange or eccentric. In short, finding out the truth about my brain has given me the opportunity to enjoy it more, to revel in its obscure architecture and peculiar lines, and to lean more heavily into my Special Interests than I ever have before.

To end this chapter on a LEGO® note, it is interesting, to me at least, that I rediscovered the joys of LEGO® just before this time of my life. Adult Fans of LEGO® (AFOL – yes indeed, there is an acronym for it) refer to the period of LEGO®-less existence between childhood and later life as your 'dark ages' – a wonderful ironic riff on the idea that the excitement and mature activities one craves in one's teens and twenties as a replacement for toys and games are somehow a bleak, poorly recorded and miserable part of one's life. Thanks to alcohol, for me this was true in a very literal sense as well as the metaphorical, but that will wait until a later, more decadent chapter than this. I left my 'dark ages' in 2013 when I noticed a new set was available on lego.com. I had stumbled across it entirely by accident, but there was no way I could feasibly pass up the opportunity of owning such a treasure: I bought myself a set based on the DeLorean time machine from the film *Back to the Future*.

Its clear cult value and sense of ironic fun meant that the 30-year-old Pete could go ahead with the purchase without feeling too foolish or childish; I had since my teenage years been so terrified of appearing overtly geeky that I had smothered it in layers of FIFA football video games and intellectual literature, an unusual mix that never quite worked but that I hoped would provide a two-layered defence against any accusations of being a nerd. The DeLorean, and the new model of the *Ghostbusters'* car (Ecto-1) a few months later, were cool enough to not attract comment. I was satisfied.

It was two weeks before I had smashed the two vehicles together in a huge fireball of ghosts and plutonium. Sprawled on the floor of my Bristol flat in my work shirt and tie, I was gazing intently at the mangled remains of both cars, my mouth involuntarily making the quiet hissing and ticking sounds of hot metal and broken engines. I had regressed, unashamedly, out of my dark ages and back into my seven-year-old sense of fun. I never looked back. By the time I had added the Millennium Falcon, *Ghostbusters* headquarters and Simpsons' family home to my collection of absolutely brilliant LEGO® sets, I no longer gave a damn about appearing to be at least slightly cool, and fully leaned into my true nerd self.

This was, looking back, my first step to discovering who I truly was, and how fitting that it would stem from my oldest and greatest Hyperfixation. By the time of writing, I have transformed my hot, poky attic room into a LEGO® utopia. It is filled (and I mean this literally) with boxes of loose bricks and completed sets, with every available space taken up with amazing models, from my large-scale *Ghostbusters* Ecto-1 vehicle to my Empire State Building and shipwrecked pirate island. LEGO® has truly leaned into its huge adult fan base in recent years and is releasing set after set after set that taps into the millennial zeitgeist. I write this modest little book with at least some hope that any proceeds may be diverted into continuing to fill up the shelves, surfaces and floor of my poky attic dwelling, and I feel absolutely no shame in this whatsoever.

Since diagnosis I am more comfortable in my own identity now than I have ever been. Having tried on many different masks and guises in my life, I find that accepting myself as autistic and also disabled has given me the greatest inner peace, ironically at a time where external events were causing more and more stress (I am looking at you, Brexit and Coronavirus). My sense of being an imposter in the autistic world has faded away, not least from the sheer volume of confirmation I get from the autistic community online that my experiences are shared by many, many people – after all, we cannot all be faking it. In the eternal fight of compassion between users of person-first language (a boy with autism) and identity-first language (an autistic boy), a huge bone of contention is the idea of autism being an identity in the same way as, say, one's gender or sexuality, or even skin colour. Many would argue that autism is not an identity – that in fact making it so makes a mockery of autism, makes it a fashionable addition to a person's lifestyle or personality. But I feel this is ableism in the same vein as how believing a person's sexuality shouldn't be classed as an integral aspect of their identity is a form of homophobia: it diminishes our own experience and our own lives, forces us to unwillingly hand over something that we *know* does shape our very being, something we *know* is fundamental to our sense of who we are, and is therefore deeply damaging. Autism is a huge part of my identity. It is written through me like 'Skegness' in a stick of rock. It is imprinted on every single one of my actions and decisions like a watermark. It cannot be set aside, and it cannot be ignored.

I am autistic in the same way as I am human.

CHAPTER TWO

My Family and Other Dinosaurs

The term *Dinosauria* was coined in the 1840s by Sir Richard Owen, the founder of the Natural History Museum in South Kensington, London. It was invented to help explain and codify the new species of reptiles that had been stumbled across for centuries but that were at this time cropping up all over the place, exposed by eager upper-class gentlefolk with aspirations in the field of geology. Early reconstructions of the animals were slow, lumbering, vapid creatures – victims of their own slothful inelegance. They were a group of organisms doomed to perish.

This chapter is about my family.

Or more accurately, it is a chapter about how family intersects with several of my favourite Special Interests – dinosaurs, genealogy and maps. What these things all share is interconnection and a sense of time passing, and what is a family if it is not a series of interconnections developing as time goes on? I suppose the visual image that acts as the glue to these disparate intrigues is the family tree – a clear diagram that maps out the connections between individuals in a way that echoes very closely the evolutionary map of life on Earth. These interrelations are fascinating to me.

However, family relationships and autism are a fraught topic: spend any time online or in conversation with an autistic person and it is very likely there will be some horror stories of their youth and the dreadful way their extended family treated them. After all, autistic people (especially when their being neurodivergent is not known to themselves or others) can struggle with these intense, close and unchosen connections with other human beings. As we are so often misunderstood by our family – and in particular our more extended family beyond the immediate safety of the domestic situation – the word 'family' when used in conjunction with jolly-sounding nouns like 'outing' or 'holiday' can cause a panic attack faster than, well, anything else. It is in the realm of aunts and uncles, cousins and nieces that being autistic becomes an *embarrassment*, either for yourself or your immediate family. They don't understand the world of autism enough, for they're not invested in it enough, and general knowledge and understanding is at such a low base level that it is next to useless. So our meltdowns, our burnouts, our stresses and strains are viewed with suspicion or outright cynicism, and going to a family birthday party at a great aunt's home can be one of the more nightmarish moments of a young autistic life. Your relatives will be either passive, calm and helpful herbivores or frightening, fast and deadly carnivores, while you are simply a goat chained to a stick in the rain.

Every child loves dinosaurs, of course. There is something paradoxically child-friendly about these unfamiliar and dangerous animals – I suppose whatever the mechanism is that makes bears suitable bedtime companions for babies is at work here – and I am not about to say that dinosaur fascination is a purely autistic trait. First, there is no such thing as a purely autistic trait (neurotypicals even stim, though to a much lesser degree compared to autistic people: what did any character do last time you saw them on TV making a difficult phone call?) and second, there are plenty of dinosaur-obsessed neurotypicals out there, and plenty of autistic folk who do not give a damn about Tyrannosaurus. But dinosaurs, like trains, are a common enough Hyperfixation and I am certain that my interest in them as a child and adult should be counted in this category. I am sure all autistic people have their own reasons for focusing on dinosaurs over, say, pigs or capybara, but I feel that there are some definite clear reasons why they are such a prominent Special Interest.

One is that they are mysterious. One cannot go up to a dinosaur and poke it. Well, I mean, you *could* go and poke a goose – after all, technically speaking (and is there anything more wonderfully autistic than 'technically speaking'?), they are avian dinosaurs, as the dinosaurs never actually went completely extinct, but I get ahead of myself. Dinosaurs are an unknown quantity as we cannot go to a zoo and watch Velociraptors prance around or Hypsilophodon prune one another. They have to, necessarily, exist in the imagination and this can be a place where autistic people excel to an extraordinary degree.

I remember having a whole bestiary of creatures in my head – in fact in many ways I have them still, they never went away, though I confess I may have gone without feeding them for long stretches over the intervening years. My imaginary dinosaurs were an amalgam of every representation of the animal I had ever seen, constantly updated as new data was fed into the software. I remember consciously having to alter my 'Plato's Cave' image of Tyrannosaurus after watching *Jurassic Park* for the first time, adjusting the stance, raising the tail, lowering the head: in all making it a far more ferocious proposition than it had been to that point. Later changes, such as adding feathers, bold colours, were similarly highly conscious and visually quite rich, in my mind's eye.

Second, they are exciting yet totally non-threatening. Many autistic children can suffer at the hands of their impressive imagination and use of fantasy worlds to inhabit when stressed, as it can lead to nightmares and terrible fears of monsters and the like. Dinosaurs, however, are wonderfully scientific, proven, known and most importantly extinct. Dinosaurs had their time, but they are gone, or at least the big scaly ones are, and they cannot flit so readily in and out of fantasy in the same way as ghosts or aliens can.

I remember being very uneasy after watching or reading any kind of ghost story; early adoption of Victorian literature (thanks, Dad) led to me finding the ghost stories of M.R. James at a relatively young age, and the more straightforward tales, such as 'A School Story', fascinated and scared me equally. The more subtle tales, such as the slow-burning 'O Whistle and I'll Come to You My Lad' (a favourite now) were a little too complex at that age, but I found enough to totally freak myself out. My father, being the keen sharer of experiences that he is, took me on a weekend trip to London when I was probably around eight or nine. This trip stands in my memory for several reasons. One is that I forgot to wear a coat for our evening zip around the underground system. I vividly recall emerging from Tower Hill station by the Tower of London itself, enthralled by the architecture of the Norman keep but shivering in my shoes in the winter air; the relief of climbing back aboard a rattling, muggy underground carriage was something I have not managed to emulate in adulthood. Autistic people reading this will recognize, I am sure, the resigned forgoing of personal comfort to avoid upsetting anyone's feelings.

The second memory is simply that late on the first night in our hotel room, we discovered *The Fast Show*, a British sketch show that fired off improbably rapid character sketches with brilliant one-liners and introduced me to the concept of comedy, something that until then I was only vaguely aware of, like the humming noise of an air conditioner. But the third memory is the key. Wanting me to experience the thrill of the West End, but being a little short of cash, my dad dragged me to the cheap theatre ticket booth on Leicester Square (I think it is still there) and managed to get us two tickets to the evening showing of *The Woman in Black*, starring Mark Curry (of *Blue Peter* fame) of all people.

Anyone who has read the book or watched the film

version starring Daniel Radcliffe will know this is an interesting move on my father's part, and to this day I suspect he just wanted to see that damn play and to hell with the collateral damage. But unless you have seen the theatrical production with your own eyes, you cannot know the absolute terror I felt in the great, draughty auditorium. The next few months of my young life were haunted by memories of the actress playing the Woman (even at this remove I feel a bit afraid that I'm being optimistic in thinking the ghost was fiction) walking the stalls' aisles, brushing past my shoulder, appearing rocking with crazed intensity on an old rocking chair behind the gauze on the stage, and appearing as a final 'fuck you' to poor Arthur at the climax of the play.

I absolutely loved it, of course – I have always been hugely partial to a good old ghost story, even as a child – but the trouble was ghosts and hauntings were *feasible*: science was unable to discount them, as far as my young self was aware. Ghosts *could* happen, whereas dinosaurs just could not. They had had their time and were now long gone, so any dalliance with the abstract idea of them was free of a dread of actually bumping into one. As such, *Jurassic Park* scared me not at all, whilst *The Woman in Black* is still the most frightening piece of media I have ever watched.

Dinosaurs are brilliant. I spent hours and hours drawing them, writing about them, reading about them, praying for the VHS of *Jurassic Park* to be released so I could finally do to that movie what I had already done to *Wizard of Oz* and *Bedknobs and Broomsticks* (that is, watch them so frequently that the tape was beginning to wear and turn grey). The most fascinating thing for me was the ways I could categorize them. Many autistic people love to be able to categorize things. Ask a room full of autists what their favourite memory of a video game is, and chances are it will be organizing their collection of axes and swords into neat little systems. Dinosaurs were my first experience of the Linnaeus system of biological categorization: I was absorbing, without realizing it, the idea that all of natural life was interconnected and related, a huge version of the more individual family trees that we all have. My favourite dinosaurs had the two-section names, too – just like members of a family, only in Latin or Ancient Greek. For every Pete Wharmby there was a *Triceratops horridus*. The most famous of these genus/species names is *Tyrannosaurus rex* – the 'rex' differentiating it from other species of Tyrannosaur, such as the much smaller *Tyrannosaurus bataar*. Tyrannosaur was the genus, the wider family of creatures. The Wharmby, if you like. Rex was the specific species – the Pete.

I saw my extended family as two very distinct genera, separated by the accident of whether they happened to belong to my mum or my dad. My mum's family was, in my youthful regard, a disparate band of smaller herds of mostly medium-sized herbivorous species. They were fairly harmless and tended to keep to themselves. My dad's family, however, were a huge herd of larger than life, ponderous sauropods, with the occasional smaller carnivore scattered about. They moved as a singular mass, grazing socially together, always chatting, always meeting, always congregating. Myself, my mum and dad, and my little sister were like a breakaway chunk of this larger herd, staying to the shadows of the edge of the jungle, ready to bolt for safety at a moment's notice.

Autism is almost certainly partly genetic in origin. We don't know much about exactly how this works, or what genes are responsible (if it can be reduced to such simplicity) and frankly many in the autistic community are suspicious of any drive to find out, seeing in it a path to pre-birth screening and a removal of autism from the gene-pool. But it seems to meander through families like a broad river, taking unexpected detours, suddenly presenting in your niece's nephew's cousin, or suddenly every member of a generation. I am autistic, my daughter is almost certainly autistic, and I am sure that my dad and sister are too – more of a direct autism canal than a river in my case. So, this little cabal of autism, orbiting the main herd of the Wharmby flock like a misshapen, slightly fed-up moon, struggled to fit in to the main group.

Growing up I inherited, mostly by osmosis, a kind of lingering unease around my extended family. They were so very different to me: gregarious, extrovert, sociable, lively – every generation of them fond of parties, get-togethers, hootenannies (I wish I were joking) and barn dances. Drink flowed, but not as a social WD40 like it was for my father and later myself, loosening up our anxieties enough to allow us to participate at all. At these parties, drink was just another fun element, like the music, the dancing or the vol-au-vents: neither necessary nor holding any darkness. It freaked me out.

It did not take long for me to realize that my little family was not like the rest of them. My dad is a typical black sheep of his family. A group of reasonably religious, rugby-loving partygoers had this youngest child – quiet, reserved, thoughtful, anxious. Born in 1954, my father had no chance of being diagnosed as autistic, and I would imagine if anyone had thought him different to his two older siblings, they would have put it down to his younger age and the fact his mother, my grandmother, died when he was only in his early teens. Since my diagnosis, and immersion in all things 'autism', I have been able to pretty comfortably identify my father as autistic, something he seems pretty happy about, all things considered, and it has explained an awful lot about my own childhood experiences, let alone his. But back in the 1960s and 1970s, when autism was an exotic and truly rarefied condition, he was on his own.

And I say this as I do not believe either of his siblings, or wider family, to be autistic at all; if they are, it is extremely efficiently masked. To be an autistic child growing up in those early days of neurodevelopmental understanding must have felt extremely lonely and confusing. But like many autistic people throughout recorded time, he did survive and make a life for himself, eventually met my mother and, presumably in a moment of optimism, decided to have children. And we were as unlike the rest of the family as you could imagine. Solitary to the point of absurdity, we had some very close family friends we would see irregularly – usually only on Big Designated Nights at their house for dinner (I particularly used to enjoy raucous evenings at Di and Gerry's house – friends of my parents from a job they'd worked at together earlier in their relationship – partly because they were so easy-going and interesting, but mostly because I adored the long dark taxi ride home down the A50 on empty roads past midnight empty fields). Watching programmes on television, such as *Keeping Up Appearances*, where neighbours would freely stroll into each other's houses to chat and gossip was alien to me. I remember regularly going to my aunt's house on Sundays with my grandad (all on my dad's side of the family) where various friends of the family would just drop in, unannounced, often to sit with a glass of wine in the kitchen. The idea of *my* parents getting visitors like that was laughable, and frankly frightening. I would not have been able to handle the random, sporadic nature of such socializing and I am sure my dad (and to a lesser extent my mum) felt the same way.

Autistic people are naturally very skittish around people outside of the immediate herd. Because we have to learn all of our social cues manually and seem to have no ability to magically and automatically discern them immediately, new people (or even known people we don't spend much time with) can cost an awful lot of energy and focus to 'learn'. This can take a very long time. I do not think I feel comfortable in someone's presence until I have known them for years, as there is always the risk of some hitherto unknown social alarm being accidentally tripped. Spending time with people we do not know inside out is inherently stressful and even unpleasant.

So it was whenever I ventured (usually without my

parents, who I think were trying to help me develop a more 'normal' range of social skills by getting me to do things they wouldn't) to one of these family gatherings by myself. I would hang like a limpet to my grandad, who although the person I knew best, was hardly the life and soul of the occasion. If for whatever reason I was separated from him, I would mill around trying to play with some cousins, slightly younger than me. Eventually I would get past the initial terrible reluctance to engage with them and slowly join their fun, but even I knew what a tortuous and lengthy process this was. The problem was, I viewed proceedings at a distance, dispassionately, in the same way a zoologist will view a colony of penguins. I always have, whenever presented with a group of people. I would identify the different sub-groups in the herd – automatically, without meaning to – and relate this to my interest in dinosaurs as a kind of natural progression. Over there were the group of uncles and grandfathers quite far removed from my line; they were a pack of intimidating Velociraptors all outdoing one another in their masculinity. Over by the doors I would spot the quiet group of great aunts, like solemn Maiasaurs – the matriarchs of the group, watchful of everything that was happening. By the bar would be the more familiar closer aunts and uncles, all chatting happily, a busy group of Gallimimus, standing and laughing and raising their glasses: friendly, approachable yet still fundamentally different to myself.

And like a herd of prehistoric reptiles, they were noisy. Chaotic. Unpredictable. I find noise challenging in all situations. As a teacher I am known for running a very quiet and subdued classroom, simply because the sound of students chattering makes me feel desperately stressed (one reason it is not an ideal job for an autistic person). If I am in a busy café or restaurant, I will find myself at times fitfully searching in vain for the volume knob to allow me to turn it all down. At a party populated by frightening individuals seemingly of a different species to me, the noise could be unbearable. Often, strangely, it was the loud music that gave me an escape – if I focused entirely on that and ignored the roars and chittering of those around me, I could ground myself slightly and find comfort in the regular beat or rhyming lyrics. If for any reason the music stopped briefly, the return to discordant pandemonium was an actual assault on my ears.

It is something we forget about all too easily when dealing with autistic people, I think – even when you are autistic yourself. The fact that we all have very different tolerances for sounds, noises and background hums, often to the point of these things causing us to have moments of absolute breakdown. The layers of noise in any given situation are something I notice very easily, and it is interesting how these layers build on one another to create a wall of sound that is unbearable to deal with. At a party like the one I am recalling – I believe it was a wedding anniversary for my aunt and uncle in a small town in rural Leicestershire – these layers of sound would be based on whatever the basic foundation noise was: in this case the mumbling sound of people chatting. Layered carefully atop this there would be the sudden, staccato drills of laughter; above that there would be the squeaks and shuffles of chair legs scraping the parquet floor and the swinging metallic sound of the door that someone keeps opening and closing. On top of *that* there would be the occasional sound of one of my younger cousins whining to their parents, and over that there would be the layer of incidental coughs, throat clearances and occasional sneezes. Throw in the odd crash of a glass breaking or the hubbub of a car alarm going off outside the village hall, and you maybe start to get a sense of what this soundscape is like for a troubled ten-year-old, out of his element, surrounded by an extended family he does not truly understand.

Because this is what it is like, and it is easily one of the hardest things to communicate to a non-autistic audience: just what it is like to have to process and attempt to filter this huge surfeit of auditory information. If I am feeling reasonably relaxed and calm, it is possible I may be able to filter out a few layers. In a coffee shop as an adult, for example, I may find myself able to ignore the hiss and sputter of the espresso machine, so long as I am not for some reason stressed or on some kind of alert. If something happens to shake me from my reverie of calm and quiet, such as my phone ringing, then all of this carefully filtered sound will crash right back into my consciousness, all of a sudden, and probably give me a headache. It is exhausting and I honestly cannot imagine how delightful it must be to not have to worry about such things.

The terrible sensory stress of these family gatherings was outweighed by the sense that these were occasions I should be attending. Our society's social code is clear, that extended family events are an absolute must, should you be lucky enough to be invited to them. I assume my parents were never actually invited – they never came with me – and as such avoided the pain of actually turning down an invitation, though I accept it is possible they were just far more capable of saying no than I was. I felt that it was a necessity to attend and tried to convince myself that enough fun and happiness would ensue to make the guaranteed stress and tension of the event bearable or even worthwhile. Autistic people do this an awful lot, I find – engage in mental gymnastics to try to justify to themselves doing something they know they will hate, like they are the opposite of a bored teenager trying to convince their parents to let them go out to the pub on a Friday night. We know what we ought to do and, because we are generally so terrified of letting people down or indeed flagging up our weirdness for all to see, we force ourselves to do it, and to hell with our own discomfort or unhappiness. Indeed, I spent the first 25 years of my life assuming everybody everywhere was in a kind of permanent state of uncomfortable misery, attending social gatherings and events because it was the *right thing to do* when deep down, they were hating every dispiriting minute. What a shock it was to discover that some people live for this stuff! They thrive in it! A different species indeed.

I found myself pushing my boundaries far, far past their usual limit when I would join my extended family on one of their yearly holidays to some far-flung outpost of the UK. Again, it was mostly out of a desire to not disappoint – in this case my grandfather, who paid out of his pocket for me to tag along with the rest of the herd. My parents never came, and nor did my sister, but it was a smorgasbord of pretty much everybody else: grandparents, aunts, uncles, great aunts, great uncles, second cousins and more, all decamped to some large holiday home in Devon or Yorkshire or the Isle of Arran or some other such bleak and windy place. Even as a child I felt a little bit like the ghost at the feast, representing as I did my strange, wilted branch of the Wharmby tree, surrounded by easily the most neurotypical people you can imagine. It was lucky that my grandfather, and by a slight extension my aunt (my father's older sister), had a fondness for me that shielded me from the majority of expectations, and I was by and large allowed to be myself on these holidays, with my tendencies towards the antisocial and arcane causing only a few rifts with other family members. But it was an essay in being endlessly and consistently out of my element – a feeling that only other neurodivergent people would recognize – a feeling of being surrounded by alien creatures with alien social rules and mores, and my most abiding memories of each of these holidays is the repetitive stream of social faux pas I committed on a daily basis.

As such I found myself, sometime in 1991, in a pub dining room in Devon. I was there with the whole gang – at least 12 of us all packed round the dark wood table, tucking into our dinners. Halfway through dinner I recall making a tearful phone call to my parents (this was the only available telephone as the holiday home did not have a landline and we were still millennia from mobile phones) where the call didn't go through properly. I don't know what I did wrong, but I could hear my parents at the other end – they had been expecting the call – but they could not hear me, and I was absolutely bereft that I wasn't heard or understood. My alarm increased and increased, as I was desperate for the familiarity of speaking with them after four or five days away. Hearing my dad put down the telephone, not knowing it was me and presumably assuming it was some cold call gone wrong, had me in floods of tears as I walked back to the table.

The trouble is, I was in 'social occasion' mode, which forbade any kind of display that might make myself an inappropriate centre of attention. I had learned very early in life that this was not the done thing, and if I were to survive in this wild world then I had to keep my head down and make as little fuss as possible. But I kept remembering hearing my mum's voice, tinny and distant down the phone, saying 'Peter?' in my head and I just couldn't hold back the tears, so I sat hesitantly, trying to look as nonchalant as possible, hoping against hope that no one would notice my silly wet face and begin the absolute nightmare of asking me what was wrong. That was *not* something I was equipped to handle at that point. Happily, though in retrospect I feel a little disappointed about this, nobody did notice, as they were all merrily chattering away. I pushed my spaghetti Bolognese around the plate, my appetite completely gone, wishing I were back home in Leicestershire, probably sitting with a mug of tea watching *Casualty* or *The Crystal Maze* or whatever was on at that time of day. I couldn't possibly eat the food I was playing with, and anyway some rogue waiter had taken advantage of my time on the phone to furtively sprinkle parmesan cheese on it so even if I had been hungry, I would never have faced shovelling it into my mouth *now* – I have forever associated parmesan cheese with vomit, and for damned good reason.

So, I did the only thing a sensible autistic boy, desperately wishing to not garner any attention at all, would do. In scenes eerily reminiscent of that *Mr Bean* sketch where he hides the steak tartare around the restaurant, I surreptitiously started dropping forkfuls of spaghetti onto the floor under my chair. Of course, I can hear you cry that this was a sure-fire way to gain some unwanted attention, but at that time I was thinking only in the extreme short term. I knew that if it had been noticed that I hadn't eaten my dinner, given my reputation (even at eight years old) as a big eater, this would be worthy of some kind of comment from someone. And it was the idea of this kind of comment – maybe a little joke, or a sarcastic dig, or a simple question whether I was ok – that was absolutely impossible to entertain. There was no way whatsoever I could handle being asked about my appetite right now and risk the whole sorry story of my botched phone call to come to light.

I wanted to keep my head down and leave this place as soon as possible, without any further interactions with the people around me. At this level of unhappiness any kind of social contact was (and still is, even now at nearly 40 years old) impossible to contemplate. I reasoned, and to this day I can totally see where I was coming from, that if

I moved the food onto the carpet, there was a pretty good chance no one would notice until the waiters did after we had paid up and left. As such, the pile of Italian food grew between my chair's legs as I continued to fight my tears, culminating in a plate that had been emptied much more quickly than any normal eight-year-old should be able to clear, even one famed for eating large portions. I glanced around at the other plates. My cousins were maybe halfway through theirs, my aunt and uncle even less so. This was a disaster. A rapidly empty plate was just as worthy of comment as a stubbornly full one. There was no reasonable means whereby I could put some of the floor pasta back on my plate – even I knew that would be a bad move – and I was dreading the sound of a voice turned to me in any perturbation. I decided to continue driving my fork around my plate, figuring that if I was lucky, no one would take sufficient interest in me to realize I was now basically playing make-believe with invisible tomato sauce.

Oddly, the gambit paid off and no attention was aimed at me for the rest of the meal. I suppose, looking back, I became a master of being unintrusive and hidden from a very early age and here I was reaping the benefits. But it was not over yet. On rising from the table, I had to push back my chair and my folly became immediately apparent – the pile of meat and pasta was right there, between my feet; a shameful pat that represented everything about me in ways no onlooker could ever realize, but that glared at me with absolute clarity. For some reason, it feels like the lights in the room were suddenly brighter and sharper than they were before. I vaguely remember my aunt spotting it, the inevitable questions, and as you may expect, the rest of the evening was spent in confusion and embarrassment.

It still gets mentioned to this day.

My behaviour was, to me, entirely reasonable. At the very least, it was logical and had a clear line of argument, and was not random, troublesome or chaotic behaviour (which is no doubt how it appeared to everyone else). But to neurotypical people such an act of dinnertime vandalism is hard to understand; we are two different species, both acting in the way we are accustomed and the way we are meant to, but to each other are as alien as two differing species of dinosaur. To a Stegosaurus, the Velociraptor's seemingly aimless running and jumping would appear completely bizarre, as it has no basis in the lifestyle of the plodding herbivore. Likewise, to a Velociraptor, a Stegosaurus' actions as it wandered slowly about, chewing bits of plant and looking thoughtful would appear confusing and unintuitive: in short, I felt more aware at that moment, and now again in typing this up, that I was of a very different species to the rest of the family, and that it was going to be very difficult to ever bridge that communicative void that existed between us.

As I grew up the situation didn't improve very much. I was always on the outskirts, looking in like a scientist might at the behaviour of any group, slightly detached and remote, though this was not intentional. Many years later I was on holiday with the family once again. It was 1998, I think – I distinctly remember Catatonia's hit 'Road Rage' playing a lot on the car radio. I didn't know it, but it would be the last quality time I spent with my grandad – I lived away from him, in another county, by this point and saw him very infrequently. He was to die a few years later in December 2000. Like any teenager, I failed to make the most of those last days together.

Once again, I felt like an alien. Every moment of every day was difficult, as if I were living in a different country and had no idea how the language worked. At the time I chalked it up to my generic awkwardness, but now I realize I was struggling with the change in routine. I have always had to deal with this when away from home. It was the same much later, when at university and frequently travelling to see friends and making a bed of their old sofas: a feeling that you are not in Kansas any more, and that things here are strange and different and hard to understand. I still have this now. Thanks to the Covid pandemic that is in its second year as I write this, it has been a little while since my last experience of this, but whenever I travel to stay with a friend or even go to stay with my parents for a few nights, I feel like a furtive foreigner trying to survive in a confusing world.

People get up at the strangest times of day.

If I go to see my good friend Nial and his wife Emma, he will invariably always wake up before me: a situation that never fails to confuse me, as the person who at home has always been the earliest riser. Emerging from the spare room to the smell of coffee and, more often than not, bacon on the grill is a tremendously confusing experience for me, despite its obvious joys. I have never gotten used to it and suspect I never will; I have also never mentioned it before now so, if you're reading this, Nial – don't worry about it! Another thing though: how on earth are you supposed to make use of any of the amenities when staying in a strange house? What are the *rules*? In my house I know how loud the shower is. I know how much water pressure it sucks from the system and whether anyone will be able to fill the kettle while I'm ablating. But in another person's house I am at a loss. At home I know how to flush the toilet – I can reliably get the thing working with one simple yank of the handle. But in every other person's house I have ever stayed at, that flush will stubbornly refuse to initiate. The number of times I have been left, twisting the handle with futile endeavour but no success, trying to be a polite and conscientious guest by removing the evidence of my toilet-time, is higher than I wish to elaborate on. Suffice to say, these days I do some practice flushes before I begin, to avoid disappointment.

In this instance, on holiday in Devon for what would be the last time with my extended family, it was tooth brushing that left me totally out of my depth. Now, I was pretty good at brushing my teeth. At 15 years old I was yet to have a filling, and I knew all the rules about not swallowing toothpaste (I didn't know why – I assumed it was somehow deadly poisonous and treated it with reverence), and how vital it was to reach around and brush the back of your teeth. I was confident. I was savvy.

Until I saw my cousins brush their teeth using a glass of water. They would brush up a thick lather of paste so they resembled the dog from *To Kill a Mockingbird*, and then take a big glass of water, swill it around their mouths and then spit it all out like a frothy fountain down the sink. Any other neurotypical child would view this dispassionately before going and doing their teeth the same old way they always have. I, on the other hand, decided that this was a Problem. This new way of doing teeth – what if it was *the* way to do it? What if I had been doing it terribly wrong for years? After all, I had been tying my shoelaces up incorrectly since I was five: it's not as if this was much of a leap. I believe I spent hours during that holiday fixated on this different way of maintaining one's dental hygiene.

I have never had any confidence in how I do things. I have always deferred to other people when I discover they do things differently as I naturally assume they have some very good reason for doing so. This might be an autistic thing, but I don't think it's directly related: more a side effect of living as an autistic person in a neurotypical world. It's hard to feel particularly confident about anything when the entire planet and the people thereon are a puzzle you can't solve. When every social interaction or experience leaves you confused and criticized, and just being alive seems to be more difficult than it has any right to be, where is self-confidence going to emerge from? And so, upon finding that my two younger cousins did this basic daily task so oddly, I determined that the only possible response would be to join them. As with everything, I decided my way must be flawed and broken.

It didn't last – I hated the sensory explosion that was swishing a load of froth around my mouth before spitting it all back out, and eventually by default I returned to my old ways, but as an illustration of how other people's domestic rites and routines would throw me off kilter, I believe it works. The whole holiday, from relaxing on the beach in Babbacombe to eating out at restaurants (this time actually consuming my food rather than leaving it in a pile on the floor), I felt out of my depth and awfully anxious. Morning and bedtime routines were fraught and scary, the etiquette of eating was confusing, and trying to take my turn to speak in such a large group of people was impossible. I was just so different to my family, so broken in comparison, so lacking confidence and self-assurance. By the end of the week, I was still far from settling in, and was very glad to get home back to my parents. At the very least, those two (and my younger sister) were pretty weird too, and I slipped back into my soothing routine quickly.

Reflecting back on this, I think these extended times out of my comfort zone got worse as I got older. I suppose when I was very young, expectations were low and not settled yet. A six-year-old finding a routine change hard is to be expected and nothing out of the ordinary. It can be chalked up to youth and happily forgotten about. But the same cannot be said for a 15-year-old. By that point, this kind of anxiety stands out vividly against expectations of how a teenager should behave. It is obvious, and therefore remarked upon. Worse, it may be challenged. Nothing had changed from my perspective, of course, but to an extended family that saw me only infrequently, my difference was clear – I was not a standard teenager at all. I was strange, odd: a different species altogether. I was a *Wharmby autisticus*. As I sit here, 20 years later, I feel bad for my teenage self. I didn't fit in. My mask, forged from years at school, was only useful in certain situations, and my ability to cope was limited. But I knew none of this beyond the gut instinct. I assumed, in my naive way, that this was life. That everyone panicked when shown a different way to clean their teeth, that everyone left food on the floor to avoid their tears being noticed, that everyone was a Hypsilophodon in a herd of Stegosaurs.

So, is it any wonder that I did what many autistic children do? I retreated into fictional worlds where such inter-species difficulties were limited to the trials of hedgehogs, foxes and human plumbers. Things were much easier in this world, where rules could be read in the instruction booklets and if anything went wrong, you could just eject the cartridge and blow on the connector to get your Sega Mega Drive working again.

CHAPTER THREE

Set Difficulty to Hard

It was Christmas 1993. The Steven Spielberg movie *Jurassic Park*, an adaptation of Michael Crichton's terrifying sci-fi classic, had loomed large in my brain for most of that year and dinosaurs were still a favourite of mine, but all of that was about to change. You see, I was about to receive my very first games console.

Video games had been a peripheral interest for years already, but had never been promoted to the premier league of distractions. This may have been due to the hardware: I had been the owner of a Commodore 64 and a Sinclair ZX Spectrum; speak of these today and geeks the world over will reply in hushed, reverent tones about the glory of these systems – their architecture, coding, the fact they were a gateway drug for a million software designers – but to me they were just too complicated. I had autistic inertia to get over, of course, and the complexity of writing in the code of a game (by no means a universal treat for autistic people) never appealed to me at all: I needed plug-and-play! This is where Sega stroll in, cocksure and spiffy in their new-found popularity based on the adventures of Sonic the Hedgehog. The Sega Mega Drive (or Genesis if you are in the US) was released in

1990 in Europe and sped to prominence over the aging Nintendo Entertainment System (NES). I had coveted one for years, relying on my weekly visits to my best friend's house on Friday evenings to get my fix of a blue speedy mammal, but now I was about to receive my very own.

We were spending Christmas in Edinburgh, house-sitting for my godmother. This had caused me considerable stress. It was my first Christmas away from home, and despite being familiar with the city I was finding being in a new environment difficult. My godmother had only recently moved to this flat, and her modernization work (installing new bathrooms, bedrooms, etc.) was very new and smelled strongly of fresh pine and paint. It was a bit of an assault on my senses. On top of this, the only television in the place was broken: the colours were wrong, as if the red tube had burned out, leaving everything odd shades of green. Knowing that I was getting a Mega Drive for Christmas, and I'd be playing through this broken television, this was a blow that I tried to absorb as best I could, with mixed success: all of the colours were going to be off. It certainly added to the anxiety surrounding everything.

Christmas can be a very difficult time for autistic people. There are, typically, a considerable number of changes to everyday routine. Gone is the steady pace of the day-to-day, and suddenly in vogue is the unexpected, the uncertain and, to this autistic ten-year-old, the downright *wrong*. Even a Christmas spent at home was tricky. The living room would no longer be what it was, decorated with what appeared to be the bizarre offspring of a winter forest and a fireworks display. Members of the family would be up at all hours, from little sister rising at 5am to father inexplicably deciding to wait until 9am to appear for the day. Morning television would be different, which may well have been the most unsettling thing (where were The Raccoons when you needed them?). But spending Christmas in this new environment, assailed by new unfamiliar stressors, was going to be an even bigger challenge. As with all things in my childhood, however, I simply took it all in my stride, pragmatically assuming that being this anxious and afraid was a normal state of affairs and that complaining about it would be a fool's errand. I was masking, even in my home, even against *myself*, guessing that I was in the wrong and that it was, therefore, my job to handle it. Pushing the anxiety down, deep down into some hidden repository of stress and terror that would eventually burst forth in a fountain of misery some 22 years later, I steeled myself for the disappointment of playing *Sonic the Hedgehog 2* with the wrong colour palette and got on with befriending the big ginger cat who roamed the halls of the place.

Making friends with this mammal was of utmost importance to me. Being a cat person, and having had Angus and Edgar earlier in life, meant I felt an affinity with all cats, whether they liked me or not. I was determined to bond with the huge orange monster despite his surly attitude and obvious disdain. It must be remembered that animals are often important to autistic people. Soothing and relaxing, they don't come with the complexity of human beings – the connotations, the implications, the snide remarks. They just *are*, rather like the video game characters I had grown to love, and this is comforting to people who struggle to navigate socializing. I made it my project to get the beast to appreciate me over the course of the holiday.

But still I was concerned about my enjoyment of my new game being dirtied by that sub-standard TV and the lack of proper 16-bit colour. The colour was going to be off. This game was important to me. It is the first time I remember feeling absolutely astonished that something *so cool* and impressive could be my own property. *Sonic the Hedgehog 2* was a smash hit in 1992 and was still selling very well a year later; it had received extremely positive reviews and was widely regarded as a masterclass in how to do the video game sequel. I had followed the news and reviews as best I could in a pre-Internet era and knew pretty much all there was to know of the game and its development. I had pored over maps of the various levels to try and work out what it would feel like to actually fly through them at hedgehog speeds and the best way to find all the elusive collectibles the game offered.

I was ready, in a way that any autistic person reading this will understand, for this game.

But the colour was definitely going to be off.

I've always found the graphics of a video game to be the most important thing. They are the best indicator of how easily I will be able to immerse myself into the world of the game, and this immersion is where my primary enjoyment lies. It is the ultimate escapism, to create your own story and inhabit your own world. Earlier games on my Commodore and Sinclair had sparse graphics – simple bright representations of basic things. But in the late 1980s and early 1990s, graphics had taken an enormous leap forward and suddenly complex scenes were possible. Colourful sprites with interesting, vibrant backgrounds brought the platform-based levels of *Sonic the Hedgehog* and similar games to life in a way that was very new to me, and I could not get enough of it. I spent hours imagining falling into these worlds. A favourite daydream was to imagine what else lay in those backgrounds, ignoring the pixel limitations and pretending there were real, detailed lives in the scenes. I longed to be able to leave the beaten two-dimensional path of a level and leap backwards into the verdant backdrop to start a new life. Such is the strong desire for an autistic person to have a safe, personal space: a world within one's mind that can be used as a sort of panic room when things get too much. Sega and their loveable mascot provided me with mine.

It turned out, in the end, that this would be such a strong desire that it would cancel out the odd colouring of my first playthroughs of the game in my godmother's Edinburgh flat. It did not matter that the colour was off. The palm trees may have been turquoise, and the red-hot lava may have been lime green but, amazingly, the game still did the job. For hours on that Christmas morning, I zoomed around the early levels, revelling in the simple joy of finally having the ability to play this game whenever I wanted. This was useful, because the stresses of being in an unfamiliar environment were taking their toll on the rest of the family too, and the traditional Christmas arguments and disagreements sparked and rumbled all day; even when not playing it, Sonic 2 was a refuge in my mind from the tension. I would be simultaneously eating my Christmas lunch and mentally playing through Chemical Plant Zone, entirely in my head and entirely for the comfort and calm that it brought me. Looking back now, I start to realize just how important this virtual safety net was for me throughout my teenage years. It would continue to be my primary means of escape for the next two decades.

I judge each year in the 1990s by the video games I played. Each year is embossed with the experience of a certain level, or character, or theme music. Nineteen ninety-four is the year of *Super Mario World* (my sister got a Super Nintendo at this point), and 1998 is the year of *GoldenEye* on the N64, a now cult console that quite frankly, I loved like a brother. These were, of course, my teenage years – years of tremendous upheaval and the horrors of puberty, which hit me relatively late but, when it came, like an oil tanker. I would move to a new house, and county, in 1997 – a change that affected me far more than I realized at the time – and I had my GCSE exams by the end of the decade, in May 1999. But it is the video games that tie everything together, and which I remember the most.

It was 1995, and I was once again struggling to stay focused in a French lesson. I attended a standard comprehensive school in a fairly deprived town in the Midlands, and French was not my forte. The teacher was a Penfold in appearance and a Baron Greenback in attitude – a terrifying, inconsistent force who never seemed to like or even tolerate me. This despite me being an unobjectionable student: I never had any desire to 'rock the boat' or draw attention to myself and as such very rarely found myself being even addressed by a teacher, let alone scolded by one. But Mr Benson had his ways. Although I was trying to focus, my brain was demanding that I pay closer attention to my thoughts on the video game I was playing at the time – *Donkey Kong Country II*, on my sister's SNES. Baron Greenback was sitting at the front of the class as I fought the desperate, biting urge to indulge myself in the comfort of my obsession with the game. I was stressed, you see. I was always stressed. I didn't know it at the time, but I was spending every day forcing myself to cope with situations that caused me extreme anxiety and even fear, and these French lessons were like nothing else. Unlike other subjects, where I could float through quietly, relying on my inoffensiveness and ability, French was impossible. I did not understand it at all; none of it came naturally to me, or even artificially. On top of that, the grim surveyor of the scene, Dr Robotnik in a cardigan, seemed to actively hate me, meaning I was always only a few moments away from being challenged in front of my peers to answer a question.

When an autistic student is stressed by their classroom environment, they have very few recourses, especially if their teacher is hostile. And autistic children find themselves to be stressed in the classroom a lot. Let us take a moment to peruse the scene, and identify the stressors, rather like an autistic driving theory test. Click your mouse when you spot the issue.

First, classrooms are too small. Baron Greenback's was

perched above the school gym, and was a tiny, boxy space with the desk up on a kind of dais at the front – a true throwback to a more frightening time of canes, pain and shame. We students were hemmed into rows of what in my head were wooden pews but which in reality were probably just very old desks, elbow to elbow, sharing all of our experiences, body heat and sweaty smells. The windows were rarely open, and the room seemed purposefully designed to capture all of the heat the school could generate, like a cannabis farm in an attic; we were not allowed to remove our thick black jumpers. And so, all of the major triggers to physical sensory oversensitivity were in place, lesson after lesson. Being too hot is probably my biggest sensory catastrophe. If I do not have a nice cool breeze blowing into my face, I am at best miserable and at worst explosive.

These days, knowing what I know about my limitations, I have a fan of some sort blowing on me almost all of the time, and especially in summer, but back in my youth I did not have this to fall back on. There's more, though: the room was filled with noise, even when the children themselves were cowed into terrified submission by the cardigan at the front. The scratching of pens across paper, coughs, creaking wooden furniture and occasional surreptitious farts would rip through the air, billowing pulses of molecules that would aim straight for my gaping ear holes, filling my brain with confusion and annoyance. Honestly, out of all of the sensory oversensitivities I have to deal with, this is the hardest to describe. As I mentioned in the previous chapter, I find it impossible to tune out sounds of any kind; if they are happening in the vicinity, my brain will be furiously making notes on them against my will, taking up a decent chunk of my available processing power.

Third, the room was filled with people and, therefore, the potential for social interaction. I have already explored how social interaction is a minefield for autistic people, but the uniqueness of a classroom in this regard is worth noting down. Due to the fact you are meant to be silent a lot of the time, school children have developed their own coded means of communication, which consists of nudges, eye contact, shared smiles and grimaces, pokes with pencils, feet tangling and kicking and even, in extreme and stereotypical cases, folded-over paper notes. Just because none of this involves spoken words, it doesn't mean there is not a danger to autistic people. In fact, in several key ways, it is even worse. The possibility of misunderstanding a vague wobble of a friend's eyebrow or the intention behind being poked in the kidney by a sharpened HB pencil is, let's face it, incredibly likely, and so you can find yourself in a mire of misinterpretation that has the ability to ruin your day. In conclusion, it is safe to suggest that classrooms like this were not happy places for me, as I am sure you can gather.

And so, my mind retreated into my video games, as a way of moderating and regulating all of this extraordinary stress. My desire to focus my attention on *Donkey Kong Country II, Diddy's Kong Quest* was borne of this, and so on this one occasion I found solace – and I mean solace so positive and peaceful that as I am sitting here right now,

I can still feel its soothing balm after all of these years –
in quietly drawing the various level maps of the game in
my French exercise book. The game had such wonderful
worlds. There was the funfair level, which featured roller-
coasters, bright lights and (in a spark of unmitigated yet
essentially random creativity) huge beehives dripping
with gloopy honey; there was the bayou level, with its
bullrushes, lily pads and echoey, swampy music; there was
the bramble level, which to this day is held in high esteem,
at least in my head, for its beauty and the quality of its
soundtrack. Drawing all of this, in pencil, in the back of
my exercise book was helping me cope with the barrage
of sensory information. It was a good feeling. The stress
was leaving me, and I was able to breathe. Until my friend
sitting next to me leaned over and said, in an outdoors sort
of voice, 'You really love that game, don't you!'

The immediate silence that crashed down could kill
a man. I blinked and turned, looking at him with something approaching despair as the grey cardigan at the
front swivelled to look at us with interest. What followed
wouldn't feel out of place in Roald Dahl's autobiography
Boy, other than that there were no physical canings – just
emotional ones. I had to move to the front of the class and
show the teacher my daubings. Now understand, autistic
doodles done as a means to regulate mood are generally
speaking not to be shared or viewed by anyone. Due to
their nature, they are often quite personal, and being
forced to disclose them to a hostile party filled me with
such dread and embarrassment I could barely maintain
my composure. My stress levels were already overflowing

– that was why I had been drawing in the first place – and this new shame was too much. As I stood there watching the man glance mockingly over my inner soul, displayed on the inside back cover of my workbook, I lost another shard of faith in other human beings.

They had been shedding from me for a few years by this point. If my faith in humanity had originally been some lovely big diamond, pure and excellent, it was now starting to resemble something you'd find if you cracked open a Casio watch. Humans were such a let-down. They drove you to absolute distraction, and then pushed you even harder over the edge. The tendency to force a meltdown upon an autistic person, and then to castigate them for acting in such a childish and ungrateful way, is a rhythm that most autistic adults will recognize and despise. At the age of 12, I was beginning to collect experiences like these, each one worn upon my psyche somewhere like an unwanted tattoo. I remember returning in shame to my desk, the back cover of my workbook removed, my head ringing with the injustice of it all. Given that this was reasonably common, it is no wonder I found the fabricated world of video games such a respite.

My taste in games was always quite fixed. Though I had some love of games that represented real-world activities, like car racing games and football games, my true love was games that had a narrative, a world of their own and the opportunity to explore. *Sonic the Hedgehog* had been like this, as had *Donkey Kong Country*. As the 90s went on, this genre became more and more impressive, offering me ample opportunity to exist in a world that was not *the* world, to be a person who wasn't me, and to be around characters who could not be anywhere near as dangerous, upsetting or plain mean as the humans in real life. The true stand-out game of this ilk at this time was the peerless *Legend of Zelda, Ocarina of Time*.

I had played the earlier *Link to the Past* instalment on my sister's Super Nintendo, a top-down perspective adventure across time and space where at one point you transformed into a lovely pink rabbit in a hat, but 1998's truly three-dimensional effort still managed to astonish me. A whole living, breathing world to roam in, with a pace all of my own. If I wanted to, I could go down to Lake Hyrule and fish all day long, or race my horse along Lon Lon Ranch's racetrack. For the very first time I had found true freedom in a video game, and I have never looked back. The real world is complex, ambiguous, hypocritical, inconsistent and vague. The world of Hyrule, with its villages, castles and volcanoes, was set, rigid, consistent and predictable: all of the things I craved as an undiagnosed autistic person, and all of the things I did not have.

The characters would always respond in the same way – conversations with them were easy and they made sense. If I spoke to one of the silvery fish people (Zora, as they are known, if you're taking notes), then they would respond with their scripted lines and nothing else. Everything was calming and expected. It was bliss. The fact that conversations in the real world, especially now I was 15 years old and more awkward than a giraffe trying to sneak out of an IKEA, were so often fraught meant that the interactions I had in these games were the most successful I had ever had. What I would give to be able to engage in the kind of talk that game offered in real life, skipping through long speeches by tapping the A button, restarting the game if I chose the wrong response, walking away if the conversation was irrelevant to me... these are dreams for a lot of autistic people, and games like *Ocarina of Time*, *Majora's Mask* (where the world was threatened by a plummeting, smirking moon) and *Banjo-Kazooie* had it in swathes.

And then there were the worlds themselves. I found the real world very stressful; most autistic people do, and I would hope that by this point you may be beginning to understand why. The real world for me in the late 1990s involved moving school, moving house and uprooting myself away from not only my close-knit circle of friends but also from a world I knew and at least vaguely understood. Coalville was not a romantic town, nor was it a particularly interesting town. It wasn't really even a nice town, but I understood it, knew its layout and more importantly where all the interesting and relaxing places were. There was the forest around the back of Snibston Discovery Park (an excellent museum showcasing the town's mining history, ironically now gone thanks to Conservative Party policy), where if you looked carefully, you could discover the ruins of an old manor house that had stood there long ago. There was the long path leading out from Townshend Lane in Donnington-le-Heath, which would eventually deposit you outside the creepiest and most fascinating abandoned detached house I had ever seen, all peeling paint and abandoned trinkets. There was the 'brook', down past the Hugglescote recreation ground, where minnows and sticklebacks and leeches could be discovered. I knew nothing of my new town, an old Anglo-Saxon redoubt squatting in the flat fenland of south Lincolnshire. It certainly didn't feel like home. So, I suppose I found surrogate worlds in my games, and they didn't disappoint.

My video game console at the time was the much-overlooked Nintendo 64. Now hugely appreciated as a cult classic, in the late 90s it was seen as a terribly uncool alternative to the laddish PlayStation, with its cool grown-up TV adverts and games about killing and driving and killing some more. The N64 was positively childish in comparison, with games such as the aforementioned *Banjo-Kazooie* – a platformer about a bear that carried a snarky bird in his backpack – seeming at first glance fit only for toddlers. But the world design was a triumph, with each themed level branching from a central hub, where secrets and Easter eggs could be found with sufficiently imaginative exploration. One thing I now attribute to being autistic was a certain paralysis when given branching routes on a video game, thanks to a fear of missing out whatever may be down route B. What treasures and treats would I miss? How will my life be made significantly less exhilarating if I take the wrong path? Is there even a right path? In open-world games like the strange bear and bird adventure, this doesn't matter. You can explore at your own pace, take every option, check every nook and cranny for the various collectable objects that are scattered across the levels. Other games, such as

Resident Evil on the PlayStation, were far less forgiving in this aspect, and become stressful to play for a person like myself; perhaps that is why I gravitated to the freedom of games on the Nintendo console. And the levels themselves were a joy to dash around in.

From memory, and I am purposefully *not* looking up screenshots on Google, there were seaside worlds with huge crabs and shark infested waters, with clattering chattering buckets and spades; there was a huge underwater cavern inhabited by a vast mechanical whale/shark creature: of course part of the level involved entering the animal's mouth, like a furry brown Jonah wearing blue shorts; the crowning jewel was the glorious season-based japes of Tick-Tock Wood, centred around a giant tree that would undergo changes to its foliage dependent on the in-game season. These were worlds that I absolutely lived inside, safe from the horrors of reality. Even after 25 years I feel residual relaxation and calm whenever I allow myself to remember these places, and I often find myself putting on their soundtracks (you can find everything on YouTube) in order to drift off to sleep.

I never successfully recreated the feeling of knowing a place like I did the town I grew up in, so this reliance on video game alternatives has continued long into adulthood. A very particular example will be explored later in Chapter Six, but all through the 2000s and 2010s I found myself viewing game worlds as alternative homes to exist in, especially in the more stressful periods. The thing is, it's not just the conversations that are set and predictable in the world of gaming: it is reality itself. Video games have certain rules that, once you figure them out, are good indefinitely; sadly, the real world does not boast this feature. Autistic people tend to find the world stressful for the multitude of reasons you are reading about here, and due to this we prefer to establish a strong, certain routine that will free up enough processing power to deal with these stresses. Having a strong routine is not some kind of highly abstract need, a need that is in some way just an oddity (and an annoying one at that) – it is an absolute necessity if we are ever going to handle everything that life throws at us on a daily basis. Having a routine is a little like putting life on autopilot, enabling us to focus our attention on the unusual and unpredictable problems that arise distressingly frequently when one is neurodivergent. This is why autistic people get so upset when their routine is broken: imagine turning off a pilot's autopilot while they are busy dealing with some kind of crisis elsewhere on the aeroplane. I would imagine that would ensue in a great deal of panicking and swearing too. But video game worlds have their own routine that is so relaxing, that it is no wonder so many autistic individuals enjoy them. In a video game, the path you should take next is always clear, or at the very least signposted.

For example, games like *Grand Theft Auto* put little glowing halos around targets that you need to deal with or head towards; in almost all games there is some kind of in-game map that will help you find your destination – imagine having one of those when you go shopping in town on a Saturday, constantly updated with the location of the seven different items you seek, showing where you are and the location of enemies (in my case, all of the other members of the public). It removes all of the variables, the uncertainty, the stress: it makes everything ordered. Most games also give you clues that something important is about to happen – a 'boss' for example, or a key moment in the narrative – as they force you to save the game or provide you with an unusually generous amount of ammunition or health. They might have a shift in their soundtrack, or the visual effects may alter in some way. Again, imagine how useful this feature would be before, say, your car got banged into by someone not paying attention in the car park, or before a large and unexpected bill arrived on your doorstep, or your disability allowance was stopped. It is a scale of organization and aid that people can only dream of, and it must be in all of this that some autistic people find solace or comfort.

The year 2000's major hit *The Sims* was an interesting and extreme example of this. It allowed my broken, autistic self to live a life unencumbered by my own understanding of how weird and awkward I was, but without the unreality of involving talking bears or speedy hedgehogs. I could set up my little avatar Sim, build them a little house and live a fairly ordinary life in a world wholly organized and set with internal computerized rules that made perfect sense. Unfortunately, the game forced socializing on us players just as much as reality does, with certain activities and career paths blocked unless you accumulated a certain number of 'friends' in the world of the game – neighbours and colleagues and such. But it wasn't so bad. In fact, it may even have helped me.

Ever since playing this game *to death* when I was 17, I have always viewed real-life social interaction through the prism of this game mechanic. The idea was that a selection of interactions were open to you that would gradually widen as you became more friendly with the other sim. You could talk, or gossip, or joke, or hug, or kiss as your acquaintance grew. The more you interacted, the closer friends you became, and any time apart would see a gradual decay of the 'bar' that summarized your friendship. I am ashamed to say, so publicly, so openly, that my internal image of a friendship in reality isn't far removed from this, and when texting a friend I do have a tendency to think of the equivalent in the game. This sounds awful, but honestly, I think it may well have saved this particular autistic kid as it served as a useful life lesson in how to maintain friendships that no adult in my vicinity would ever have bothered to share with me, seeing it as so obvious to their neurotypical sensibilities.

The Sims has a dedicated autistic fan base, with new instalments (I believe we're up to *The Sims* 4 by this point) fervently discussed and scrutinized, and I am not surprised by this. Here is a game that explicitly teaches you how to do life – how to get a job, keep a tidy home, the pitfalls and dangers of ordinary adult life. I am genuinely pleased I had my toilet get blocked in the game, or my oven break down and set alight, as these were valuable little vignettes that prepared me for the bleaker moments of adulthood. Adult autistic people can find the daily grind of life very hard to manage, usually because so little of it is explicitly explained, and this game mitigated this a little. Perhaps it should be part of the curriculum for autistic students in school – it certainly did me far more good than those lessons dedicated to learning when you are legally allowed to buy a pet, or vote, or whatever. And even past the incredibly useful life lessons offered, the simple order and rules of the gameplay managed to keep me pleasantly relaxed.

I would typically play the game (and all my others) after school – often immediately after getting through the door. I'd be exhausted from masking – putting a facade of nonchalance over my anxiety and fear of everything – and desperate to 'unwind' which, as terms go, is pretty much literal in its description of how autistic people feel when they manage to relax. For me it is a very physical feeling, like I am unfolding myself somehow, opening back out again after being tightly furled like an old handkerchief for the whole day. These games offered a way to do this unfurling a little more quickly and effectively, and the tasks and objectives they set for us calmed and soothed in various ways.

Out of all of the various types of gameplay that exist in video games, the best for me was *repetition*. In gaming circles, we call any repetitive task that gradually awards the player in some way the 'grind', and it is something that my autistic brain views with reverence. The thought that by doing a basic task, many times, you can gain the upper hand in some way – find any kind of benefit – is intoxicating to me and makes me inordinately happy.

When I was 14, I discovered *Pokémon*. The original game, with its 151 strange little critters, had been available in Japan for about a year and had just arrived on European shores. To begin with, being the only human being in the UK not to have a Nintendo Game Boy, I had to appreciate the phenomenon from a distance, but then a spin-off game called *Pokémon Stadium* appeared on the N64, with a special implement that enabled me to play a Game Boy game through that console on my television. I was very happy.

For those who are not familiar, *Pokémon* puts you in the position of training these strange animals that you can catch, turning them into little fighting machines. It's a cute virtual version of dog fighting, only with much less blood (Pokémon simply faint when defeated, like a Victorian heroine). But to get your creatures to be the very best, like none ever were, you must perpetually send them to battle others. Over and over again. Each battle awards a tiny amount of 'experience', the accumulation of which allows them to 'level up'. For many players, this relentless repetitive activity is too boring, and the rewards too pointless, to be attractive. Not so for me. I approached this grind with gusto, revelling in the fact that time spent on such a routine, safe and easy task would yield benefits. As such, by the time I reached the first 'boss' in the game – a stalwart young pervert called Brock – I had managed to train my team of beasts to absurdly high levels and absolutely annihilated the poor fellow. The rest of the game was just as easy, and I loved every boring minute of it.

After all, a lot of autistic play is repetitive in nature, and I believe this is thanks to a desire to instil calm and order into a chaotic world. It is often cited as an early sign that alerts parents and teachers to possible neurodivergence – for example a young child repetitively lining up their toys or doing the same jigsaw over and over. This is fine – anything that enables an autistic child to get themselves diagnosed speedily is great – but sadly it is not always viewed in a positive way. Any hint that a child is playing with their toys in an unexpected way can trigger a terrible storm of attempted modification of their behaviour.

Autistic children worldwide receive this kind of treatment very regularly. To understand it, imagine a left-handed person going through years of torment from their teachers and parents, effectively having right-handedness beaten into them over years. This is an insistence on conformity and is extremely common – folk hate difference, after all – and autistic people have it done to them very frequently, only with a much broader focus on a much broader set of behaviours. Lining up our die-cast cars in lovely, interestingly ordered rows is one of these behaviours that can face attempted eradication if no one steps in to prevent it. Practices such as applied behaviour analysis (ABA) exist mostly to medicalize this, and in the process torture and traumatize large swathes of the autistic community, as they encourage children to eschew their natural coping mechanisms (such as stimming) in favour of more socially acceptable ways (such as bottling it all up until you explode in fury in your late teens). This is often achieved by withholding praise and toys as a kind of punishment for not conforming. It is hard to be surprised when one learns the process of ABA was invented by Ivor Lovaas, the pioneer of homosexual conversion therapy.

Everything autistic people do to find solace, comfort or enjoyment can be pathologized by malevolent forces out to make a quick buck. This is the sad reality we exist in at present, and yet another reason why these make-believe worlds, packed with cartoon fun and established routine, feel like a safer place to exist than the grim, ableist reality. Grinding through the levels of *Pokémon* was a safe, secure and predictable world that offered a great deal more than the rest of the world appeared to.

Back to the game, the mathematics of *Pokémon* appealed a lot to my autistic brain too. Now, I cannot for one second bear the lazy stereotype that autistic people are all maths wizards – we most certainly are not, and my grasp of it is tenuous at best, but the simplicity of the numbers game was elegant and straightforward, at least in the first few games (later instalments got very complicated). The paper-scissors-stone mechanic of which types of creature could nobble others the most effectively was logical and easy to remember and, above all, fully consistent. Electric-type moves were very effective against flying-type, or water-type, which made perfect sense to me because of, well, lightning and so on. Similarly ground-type worked very well against electric, so bye-bye Pikachu if the other side is rocking some kind of weird tiny mole creature with 'Earthquake' as an attack. Working out strategy from this very basic starting point was surprisingly rich and complex, and my reveries during lessons by the time I was working on my GCSEs were increasingly based around this game and working out perfect teams of six little critters to be able to handle any eventuality. I'm surprised

I managed to pass any of my exams, given how much time I diverted to this. But it was worth it. Sure, the graphics were dreadful and the music beepy and repetitive, but the experience of playing *Pokémon* was out of this world. I'm not sure I've ever experienced anything quite like it. Nowadays I play the frightening modern and impressive *Pokémon Go* on my mobile phone (another game that has a huge and dedicated autistic fandom) of course, and it is great at what it sets out to do. However, it has never quite reached those dizzying heights of joy that the late-90s iterations managed.

As time crawled by, my love of video games endured. I have dedicated a whole chapter (Chapter Six) to one of them, which dominated my life for a period in the 2010s, but most of the last few years have been focused on the heady thrills of online competitive play. These are games that endure, where all achievements are remembered and every single thing you do is recorded and counts for some kind of player growth. Obviously, for someone enraptured by the simple growth system of *Pokémon*, this is beyond addictive – and addiction is the problem. I don't think autistic people are more prone to addictive personality than other neurotypes, but I can say it may be harder for an autistic person to extricate themselves from the addictive cycle once it begins. This raises an intriguing and important question: what happens when a Special Interest goes bad in this way?

Because a favourite interest has such a soothing, balm-like effect, it can be hard to summon up the willpower to extricate yourself from it once you realize things are becoming increasingly toxic. The problem of the addiction against the soothing effect of the activity can be a difficult equation to balance. Video games are addictive as they trigger brain hormones in a similar way to gambling (and often the line is extremely blurred – see slot machines and mobile 'gacha games'), meaning a feeling of positive achievement can be chased, to the detriment of the individual. And online play offers this to a fault. The buzz of defeating a human opponent, as opposed to a clumsy construct controlled by the hapless computer, is huge, mostly because it is so much more difficult to achieve – it is easy to fall into a loop of time-sapping misery if you're not careful. Shooting games like *Counter-Strike* are whirlpools of time and energy, sucking in every moment of your life, even when working or ostensibly asleep. The virtuous cycle of the interest feeding and restoring ends up inverting, until it leaves you exhausted and unfulfilled. If I sound battered by this, it's due to my years of experience of falling into this pit, clambering out only to comically tumble back in again.

The positive feeling of vanquishing an enemy (who is likely to be a ten-year-old in Turkey) is such that it's possible to convince yourself that it is all good, that the echo these victories give you of that lovely warm feeling from childhood – that ruined, half-forgotten remnant of how happy *Banjo-Kazooie* made you feel – is legitimate and truly positive, even though it is only a ghost.

Online competitive play is the kebab of gaming: moreish, delightful for around 15 minutes and then causing a period of emptiness and despair that lasts for the next six hours. It's all empty calories that leave you craving more.

I have found myself in this trap several times, getting increasingly irritated by the fact that playing against human competition is so much more difficult than facing artificial intelligence. Humans are wily, quick, unpredictable and attuned, and unless you have spent years honing your skills, you are unlikely to be able to effectively challenge them. But this didn't stop me: the worst thing about this situation is how it turns the grind – that best friend for so many years – against you. In a game like *Pokémon* or the medieval fantasy epic of *Skyrim* it is a real joy, relaxing and soothing. But the grind in multiplayer is horrible. You only gain benefits from long periods playing and winning, but this is enough to draw me repeatedly into the Charybdis. I spend hours desperately trying to level up – not certain why it's so important but with absolute focus. Every loss is an impediment to my progress. Every win is a little boost.

These games have, in effect, weaponized my love of gaming against me. They have expertly laid out what attracts me to gaming, like a delicious buffet packed with cake and those little sandwiches, and then proceed to hide those little sandwiches behind barriers that only a considerable amount of time and – in many cases – money will remove. In all honesty, I am a sitting duck for this kind of dodgy practice; my proclivity for obsession – so benign in so many cases – turns to something more sinister and unpleasant: I end up addicted to a game I do not even enjoy.

This has happened many times, and each time has added to the accumulated damage. Looking back, I can identify the online modes of *Red Dead Redemption* and *Call of Duty: Modern Warfare* as the earliest culprits, with *Call of Duty* being by far the more insidious. I played the hell out of the online multiplayer mode of that game, and I'm not convinced I enjoyed a single second of it. But the grind of gaining 'xp' and unlocking little treats every now and then captured me completely. Later it was the *FIFA* football games that ensnared me, with their nefarious 'Ultimate Team' mode which functioned as a playable version of those football sticker collections that were popular in the mid-1990s. I would play to earn online currency to open 'packs', hoping to get some rare and high-quality footballer (and never doing so, of course – the odds are extremely low), and then use my new players to play more to open more packs.

As feedback loops go, it is simple but dangerously effective, especially considering the ability to take a shortcut and buy in-game currency with actual real money, from your actual real bank account. And this is a game aimed at children; it's little wonder the media is always reporting stories of parents peeved by their child spending £4000 on their credit card on imaginary football stars. But the saddest thing about this whole charade as far as I was concerned was this: I absolutely hated playing the actual game itself and was only hopelessly fixated on the gambling of the pack opening. Thus, the grind of playing matches for currency was an experience of total misery and frustration.

I include this to show the flip side to the joy of autistic interests and to illustrate how readily and easily they can backfire on us. A savvy game developer, knowing about human psychology, can forge a game that taps into the neurotypical brain with ease, without even realizing that the same techniques work 30 times more successfully on neurodivergent people. There are no research studies into this – why would there be? There's no money in it – but I would be fascinated to see how many people addicted to the most modern and efficient iteration of this type of game – the smartphone game app, like *Candy Crush* and *Marvel Strike Force* – are autistic or otherwise neurodivergent in some way.

There is time left to give a final example of the dark flip side of this Hyperfixation. The result of prolonged gaming of this (or any) type on my brain can be quite unpleasant. If I spend too long on a game in one sitting (anything above, let's say, three hours), I start to dissociate from reality. Not in the good way of being immersed in the game world – that wouldn't be a problem, is usually my aim in the first place and is no different to being immersed in the fictional world of a novel – but more a total disconnection from reality and life itself, as if you've become a disinterested observer of events rather than taking part. I begin to feel anxious, untethered: like a hot air balloon that has lost its anchor and is being carried wherever the wind wishes. It is a deeply unpleasant sensation and is not limited to video gaming – it can occur if I spend too much time on other interests. Most recently it occurred when the Swedish band ABBA reformed (the best news we've had since the pandemic started) and released a couple of new songs. My brain slipped into a 'I must now know everything about ABBA' mode and, eight hours later, when I emerged from the Internet feeling sick and lost, looking at my surroundings as if I'd never seen them before, I barely even recognized the legitimacy of my own thoughts. It was a very strange feeling, and is a reason why I always have to be careful when allowing myself time to enjoy my interests.

But then I have long tended to get sucked into the world of music, with its personalities, stories, ideas, relationships and histories. In fact, for a period of around ten years, it was the only thing I really cared about, as we shall see.

CHAPTER FOUR

Come Together

I do not know what my taste in music is. For a very long time I knew what I *wanted* it to be, as I was aware (especially in my late teens and twenties) of what music was deemed worthy, cool or acceptable, and for most of my adult life I have mistaken this knowledge with taste. Now I approach 40, though, I am beginning to realize that this understanding of the fashions of music is not a very good replacement for being aware, comfortable and confident in your own favourite tunes.

I have asked many other autistic people about this, and about the sister issue of 'What's your favourite film or television show?' and the responses are often very similar: a real lack of confidence in explaining our likes and dislikes, and a complete inability to identify a small number of things we can happily state are somehow better and more important to us than any others. As time ticks on I am increasingly of the opinion that having 'favourites' of anything is a distinctly neurotypical position to hold, but I am aware this angle may veer into the controversial. As far as I am concerned, some music is good, in that I enjoy the feeling of listening to it, and other music is bad, in that listening to it is either boring or stimulates no emotion whatsoever. I suppose that some music could be identified as having a bigger emotional impact than others, or that some might sustain how pleasing they are to my ear for longer, but beyond that an ability to pick a favourite is beyond me. But that is fine as far as I am concerned.

For me, music is a way to moderate my mood and energy levels; in certain ways it acts like a non-intrusive and fairly harmless medication and fulfils very much the same role as physical stimming in regulating my stress levels, so long as I remember to listen to some when in the throes of pre-meltdown. This is how I entered the world of music, listening to my old cassette tape of *Now That's What I Call Music 10* back in 1992 or so, letting the chilled-out guitar and electronics of 'Crockett's Theme' by Jan Hammer soothe me better than anything else I had ever found – even the video games I had been playing on my Sinclair Spectrum. But because I only really used it as a way of relaxing, I had no insight into the fashionable side of music, no desire or drive to seek music out or actively pursue it in any way. Like so many things, being autistic seemed to mean that a sense of terrible inertia spread into everything – even areas where you might reasonably expect me to be more active. It is too easy to get sucked in by the comfort of the familiar, and as such my taste in music was entirely (and boy do I mean *entirely*) led by my parents' obsession with 1980s electro and New Romantic stuff. Before my birth completely messed up their ability to go out and have big nights out, they had been real music obsessives, and clearly this rubbed off on me, only in this peculiarly passive way.

The music of my childhood up to the age of maybe 15 was *all* that of my parents. The only exception I can think of to this was a brief obsession with the Mr Blobby single from around 1994, but despite this book being very heavy on the personal details I cannot allow myself to go into more detail about that. Until my purchase of *The Man Who* by Travis, the only music I listened to was from the late 1970s and the 1980s – bands such as Adam and the Ants, Erasure, Pet Shop Boys and going a little further back, ABBA. I remember babbling at school to my friends about a VHS I was watching daily of Adam Ant's biggest singles and their videos (think 'Prince Charming' and its famous jerky dance or dandy highwaymen and their white paint-swept faces) in the same way a more 'switched-on' 11-year-old might have discussed Nirvana in the playground of the time. Naturally, my friends had no idea who or what I was talking about; it wouldn't take long before they were getting an interest in the Spice Girls, Take That and Boyzone: you know – bands that were still actually together. I was aware of these outfits but didn't actually hear any of them until either my mum or my sister got interested in them: as I said, I was passive to the last.

In all, this forms a strange start for a Special Interest, but looking back this seems to have been often the way for me, and I believe it all to be linked to this idea of not having the confidence in my own opinions, fearing that in some way I could not possibly be qualified enough to even *hold* an opinion on something as vast as music; the fact is I built a decent-enough façade of a taste in music to get me through – more masking in order to feel part of the 'real world'. It was through television, and more specifically the music channel MTV2, that I gained the insight I needed to be confident enough to talk about music that was new and cool. Much like how I had built up an instruction manual of social behaviours by carefully observing the actions of those around me (attentive readers will remember this from Chapter One), I managed to construct a portfolio of opinions on music based on the behaviours I observed through this alternative music channel, plus printed media such as the *NME*, *Q Magazine* and (looking back this amuses me enormously) the music fan pages of Ceefax and Teletext. I was so utterly captivated by this slow-refreshing terrestrial TV-based proto-internet that a genuine worry I had just before setting off to university was how I would cope without it once I was in student halls and lacked a TV with an aerial connection.

Despite having this newfound wealth of opinion and information to draw from, being completely naive, I took every single opinion I read as being somehow sacrosanct and the definitive word on the subject. I quickly learned that there was something extremely sacred about Nirvana's *Nevermind* album, even if you never listened to it; that R.E.M. were great but mocking them was generally acceptable; that there was something weird about Smashing Pumpkins that no one could quite put their finger on, and finally that *OK Computer* by Radiohead was the finest album since *Let it Be*, or *The Bends*, depending on who you listened to. As an example to my unfounded faith, I totally accepted the furious, feverish excitement that accompanied the release of Manic Street Preacher's sixth album in 2000 (*Know Your Enemy* – the one with the sad song about fruit juice) and took people at face value when they publicly wrote that the song, now essentially forgotten, 'Intravenous Agnostic' (and is there a more Manic Street Preachers song title than that?) was quite simply the best song ever written. This was, I realize now, a very autistic trait: to accept someone's words as completely unencumbered by exaggeration or overenthusiasm, to believe that if someone was willing to write such extreme things, they must have given it due diligence and proper thought and would, therefore, be a reasonable and important take. If it were written down, I seemed to reason, then it must be true. This trait would cause me problems throughout my long love affair with music; I never seemed to learn and continued to fall foul of others' hyperbole. But amongst all of this I absorbed the information like a desiccated sponge, feeling that I had a lot of catching up to do.

I was 17 years old and even I was aware that most teenagers' musical renaissance had already happened by this point. As is so frequently the case for autistic people, I was a late bloomer, but soon caught up (or at least put up the pretence of catching up) thanks to my borderline obsession with reading everything I could about music. This was the start of an eight-year period where my other interests, so carefully exposed to you here, were put on hiatus. LEGO® fell away completely, as did war gaming (see the next chapter). Video games survived (but only just) and faced some real friction from some of the people in my life at that time, who saw that particular hobby as wasteful and pointless. I think I pretty much forgot the *Titanic* even existed for a while, and dinosaurs... well, dinosaurs were extinct.

Once I had learned the lingo and trends of alternative music, it became the greatest social lubricant I had ever experienced. This eight-year period of my life from age 18 to 26, where music had total primacy, was easily the most sociable period of my life. Every friendship I made at this time (and these are the friendships that have endured to the present) was based in some way or another on music, either the creation or the appreciation of. One has a love of 1980s electro music at its core, while another is at least partly built around a regard for bands like the Libertines, the aforementioned Manics and Dave Grohl's Foo Fighters. It feels to me that to be autistic is to want friends, to need friends, but to lack the language of friendship in some strange way. As uncomfortable as I am describing anything to do with autism by nouns like 'lack', I cannot see it any other way: something about the way friendships work eludes me, and music helped patch over that gap with startling efficiency. Needless to say, I had more friends over that period than I have had before or since, and the idea of somehow being able to replicate that now I am in my late thirties, sullen and bowed by depression, seems darkly laughable. It was a time of gigs, parties, nights playing poker at strangers' homes, evenings in the pub and rehearsals. It was probably the closest I have ever got to what I can sometimes see, in my more miserable moments, as a real life.

Music is great for autistic people though. Like TV shows and film, it carries messages, stories and lessons that can help us assimilate and fit in to the neurotypical world. Everything I know about drug culture, for example, I know from music, from Pulp's *Sorted for Es and Whizz* to Guns 'n' Roses' *Mr Brownstone*. The importance of this cannot be overestimated: autistic people can truly rely on these narratives to cope with the complexities of life and society. Autistic children are taught about life through Social Stories™ – cartoon strips that help explain social interaction – and we absorb from pretty much every narrative presented to us.

Music, and specifically the lyrics of favourite songs, can help you manage jealousy (*Mr Brightside*, *Jealous Guy*), loneliness (*Help!*, *The Visitors*) and fury (*Bullet with Butterfly Wings*, *Karma Police*). And it can be such a stimming tool! I'm a reluctant dancer – other than a brief and deeply misguided period in my third year of university, where I decided that throwing the most extreme and energetic shapes was the most likely way to get me noticed, I have essentially *never* danced publicly – but if I am alone and have music playing, moving along to the rhythm with my toes and hands is a terrific way to de-stress, as I guess it must be for all autistic people. It is a way of blocking out the world too. Lots of autistic people like to wear ear defenders to reduce the audio glare of the world around them, but wearing decent noise-cancelling headphones with your favourite music playing is far superior to this, in my view. Walking through a crowded shopping street with Manic Street Preachers shouting about being architects and pioneers in my ears is a perfect way of managing to avoid the throngs of people, even though they are still technically there. The music lifts me away from all that and makes it transitory and irrelevant. I appreciate music very much for its ability to do that.

In fact, there was a time that forgetting my headphones when going for anything from a walk to the shops to the train to Edinburgh would be a disaster beyond imagining. I was at university during the death throes of the compact disc era, and on long train journeys I was never apart from my Sony Discman (a portable CD player with non-skip technology: this tech was of supreme importance, I recall, when we compared our players, much like the waterproof-to-so-many-metres accolades that posh wristwatches boast. Mine had a four-second non-skip function, which meant it would continue to play even if I were tobogganing down a mile of corrugated iron in a tin bath; I was proud of that). I would carry around a large selection of CDs with me, everywhere I went, including their cases. There was no way I would risk having them loose in my bag – what's the good of a four-second non-skip function if all your disks were scratched to hell? – so I would resign myself to the fact that any other luggage or essentials, such as clothing, toiletries, set texts for my English Literature degree, would be minimal in number and tiny in nature to allow for me to bring the entire oeuvre of Weezer and Radiohead to Newcastle, or wherever in the UK I was heading.

The advent of the iPod, which for me occurred in 2006 when my parents bought me one for Christmas, no doubt aware of the terrible strain I was putting on my lower back, changed my life forever. At the time I was working at an independent first aid training company led by a manic individual who would show me how adept he was at martial arts by lowering his pulse rate at will. 'Mind over matter', he would chuckle at me – possibly the least interested individual he could share this with – before going to crash his car for the fourth time that year. This was the kind of job where I had enormous amounts of free time, which would be spent cooking up arcane lyrics. The iPod helped with this a great deal. Suddenly I had the ability to truly immerse myself in whatever music took my fancy and listen to it whilst walking to and from work. My musical buddy Tom, an old school acquaintance who had become a good friend after we left, with whom I lived in a tiny old student house 'uphill' in Lincoln, would periodically steal my device to upload a random selection of tracks that I would discover the next day. It made my daily shuffle very exciting, knowing that my old favourites (which at this point included a lot - and I mean a *lot* - of Michael Nyman and ragtime piano) would be interspersed with new stuff that I would happily imbibe as I strolled down Wragby Road. Nowadays I am very unhappy about trying to enjoy new music, set in my ways as I am as both an autistic and a middle-aged man, but at that point I was in heaven.

I needed music. Looking back, it was easily and by far my most all-consuming Hyperfixation I have had to date. Any moment I spent not listening to it or creating it was a moment wasted, and my other interests waned and faded in its bright glare. It was natural, I suppose, that I would find myself in making music after this crash course in musical culture. After all, I had taught myself guitar from the age of 18, playing a nice if highly aggressive acoustic, which was something of a turn-up for the books as far as my parents were concerned. Up to this point my entire musical education had consisted of one lesson learning to play the flute at primary school (I quit because they expected us to write a tune as homework – I couldn't even make it make the right noise) and a period of over-ambitiousness with a glockenspiel at secondary school, gleefully banging out twee versions of TV theme tunes during our double periods of music.

Suddenly deciding to learn the guitar took everyone by surprise, including myself, but it was an obsession that simply wouldn't go away. I did not bother to learn music – I still cannot read it – but I took the time to understand guitar tablature, which is a highly simplified yet really useful surrogate. A grand total of zero formal lessons later, I found myself able to form chords, string them together, keep a rhythm... eventually even sing a little while I played, so long as I wasn't too precious about keeping time. Hooking up with a like-minded individual to create our own tunes was going to happen: it was simply a matter of time.

Playing an instrument made a great deal of sense to me from the off. There is something impeccably logical about making your way around the neck of a guitar that appeals to me enormously, despite the fact the underlying musical theory feels totally nonsensical to my brain. My brain works in patterns, so the repetitive, Tetris-like webs of chord shapes and scales psychologically printed themselves on the lacquered wood very quickly. I found enormous relaxation and even solace in these patterns, to the point that it approached a form of synaesthesia. I have elements of the more traditional synaesthesia – seeing odd numbers as being cold, blue and harsh purple, whilst even numbers are warm greens and oranges – but to me chords on a guitar had very different textures or consistencies. A G chord felt smooth yet angular, whilst a D chord felt childlike and bouncy, like a plastic toy in my hand. An E minor felt blunt, sullen and obstinate like a rock you might find on a beach: all of this helped me memorize chord progressions and songs, as I was essentially just lining up different-shaped objects and recalling their order. I don't feel I ever mastered the guitar, but I got reasonably proficient at it at a reasonable pace and found myself fulfilling the role of rhythm guitarist in prototype sessions with my friend Tom as we began messing around with creating tunes. Far from being anything approaching a 'band', for a long time it was just the two of us – I would write lyrics in the little red book I lugged around everywhere, sending little emailed care packages of them over to him from my university library, so he could pair them up with one of his excellent new melodies.

Occasionally we would get together whenever I went home for the university holidays – often somewhere strange or even unnerving, like the cold dark Coronation Channel that cuts through the back of Spalding as a way of absorbing floodwater to protect the flat lowlands, or a tall dyke along the river Welland near a rarely used country track at midnight – to practise playing these songs. I'm not sure exactly why we gravitated to these silent, remote spots, but I feel it was a defence more than anything: a desire to stay firmly away from the rest of humanity when we were in a vulnerable state – because that's what writing music causes: extreme vulnerability. I can't speak for my friend of course, but from my point of view trying to vocalise these new songs was extraordinarily difficult. I'm not a natural singer – not by a long way – nor did I ever intend to actually be a singer. I suppose the position ended up mine by default. But I had no confidence, and though these very early, windswept sessions ended up yielding some very good music, I continued to find it very difficult, which never truly went away. And I was not very good at communicating these difficulties.

❖

Autism is all about communication. Well, to be clearer, difficulties of communication. Failed communication, such as taking a joke seriously, taking a deadly serious utterance as a joke, missing sarcasm, taking banter person-ally, misinterpreting instructions or expectations... these things leave us battered and emotionally bruised, which can lead to a gradual shutting out of the social world. Why would anyone willingly put themselves out there when the expected results are so painful and traumatic? Much easier to eschew human contact as much as possible and relax in the quiet calm solitude of a life alone. I had already begun to float along this route towards the end of my time at university; having made a few firm friends, the rest of the social experience was too exhausting for me, and I had no desire to expose myself to any more of it. My university experience was filled with people – those I shared classes with, sat next to, sporadically chatted to – but probably 90 per cent of them are nameless in my memory now; my extant friends from the time will mention them in passing when reminiscing of our youth but none of their names ring any bells at all. I sometimes wonder if I wandered around my university department with my eyes closed; if I had been an inveterate drug user back then it would have made more sense, but in the total absence of that I think I just cut myself off absolutely from the bulk of the people around me. Better to huddle in a quiet corner and watch the world go round than put myself into a situation where any unwanted attention might glue itself to me like one of those sticky long weeds that we used to chase each other with at primary school.

As a result of all of this, I did a very sensible thing, and during my final year Tom and I formed an actual band, based on our earlier musical forays. Looking back, I am not entirely sure I properly thought this particular decision through. Like so often in my life, executive dysfunction (the autistic and ADHD trait whereby planning, prioritizing and keeping track of things is very difficult) reigned supreme and the consequences in this case (for example, having to go on stage and perform music, to other people) were far off and vague; it was something to deal with at a later date. We would cross that bridge when we came to it. All that mattered was that I be in a band. It was the natural way to advance my obsession with all things musical: it was either that or enter the world of musical theatre. From this point on, the band and creating its music (or specifically writing lyrics) became the number one aspect of the music obsession – a true Hyperfixation that provided the battery for around five years of high-energy effort and achievement. Throughout it all, and I cannot stress how important this is to understanding how our monotropic interests can drive us, I remained just as autistic as I had been as a child, and just as autistic as I am now, typing this filled with anxiety, with a fan blowing cold air into my face despite the fact the temperature is only just into the low 20s, overthinking the phone call I had earlier with my agent. Despite being autistic, and I believe in this case the negative conjunction is justified, I pushed through all of these difficulties *thanks to* the effects of Hyperfixation: the way it seems to provide strength, energy and capability.

However, there is much about autism that does not suggest that being a lead singer in a rock band is a great idea. The noise is perhaps the most obvious thing; the unbelievable volume of speakers, amplifiers and drums on stage can't be overstated. Even with ear plugs it is a din that is quite different to the sound the lucky punters hear, and it is genuinely a wonder that I managed to cope with it at all. This can be followed by the high expectations of social engagement – so much schmoozing, chatting, flirting, charming and so on and so forth, and that was just with the drummer.

But it is more than just that. What about the leadership? The taking charge? The organization? All of these are traits any decent leading man should have in some abundance, but they are not traditionally seen as the strengths of an autistic person. But I did as much of it as I could, as have many other autistic people – some who have achieved great fame. Courtney Love, for example, the lead singer of the band Hole, has a lifetime of what could be described as stereotypical 'rock-star experiences'. Gary Numan has made music for a very, very long time. When my band was starting out, the *NME* was regularly packed with tales about Craig Nicholls, lead singer of the Vines, who was openly autistic: possibly the first exposure I had to accounts of an autistic experience. Being totally unaware of my own neurodivergence at this point, I simply saw it as an interesting bit of trivia; now I see it as something rather more important. It is one of those common paradoxes about autism, in that it should not work, but it does.

Then there is the anxiety of autism – that all-encompassing, endless grind of fear that overwhelms at times – which does not mesh well with the extra anxiety of being on stage, of performing, of laying your soul on the line by daring to sing in public. But then when you live a life of endless, crushing anxiety, what's adding another layer? What extra harm can it possibly do? After all, for so many autistic people, living around other humans is a performance anyway: why not make it a musical one too? There are other positives though, that begin to balance the issue: there is a physicality in music that many autistic people might enjoy. Though we are by and large a group sensitive to sound, there is a kind of threshold where noise goes from being awfully loud and terrible to pleasingly loud and amazing. Please don't ask at what decibel this magical transformation occurs; suffice to say it does, and that being on stage with a wall of amps vibrating every molecule of your being can be a splendid experience for an autistic person. Eccentricity is accepted, even lauded in the musical world, and front-men are allowed to be aloof, distant, quiet-when-off-stage and rude. This was perfect camouflage for me; I could be myself and no one would bat an eyelid. Perhaps this is how I managed it.

Our songs were short, punchy numbers, carried along by our drummer's intensity and ridiculous pace, but as I was responsible for lyrics, the songs were about pastoral, almost Romantic themes – imagine if Wordsworth had been in a heavy garage band in the early 2000s and you may get close to the reality of our songs. They had titles like 'The Forest Song', 'Cloud Shadow on Dover Beach' and 'Night Air', and the odd disconnect between lyrical meaning and musical clout was, I suppose, one of our biggest selling points. As we played, our ambition grew and I found myself in increasingly tenuous situations, where my natural social phobia and high anxiety levels would spike on a regular basis. Though getting on stage was terrifying to begin with, I gradually warmed to it; the problem was chattering afterwards with other bands, audience members and even my own bandmates: this was the scarier thing. I survived by playing the disinterested front-man card over and over again, my nonchalance masking a turmoil or worry inside.

As you might expect, anxiety gripped my entire

existence as a member of a band. Every gig we played, my brain would fixate on something to worry about. In Oxford, it was whether the bass player would arrive by train on time for our set (he arrived with over an hour to spare). In Leicester it was whether I'd forget all the lyrics to the songs I had written (in my defence this had happened already, a few months before on BBC Radio Lincolnshire – I was reduced to dooby-dooby-dooing for a whole verse as the words had vanished from my mind). In Lincoln it was whether I would actually fit on stage, as there was a kind of balcony above and I'm rather tall. On that instance I did have to remove my shoes in order to stand up straight by the microphone, so I suppose my anxiety on that instance was reasonable. But all too often it was baseless, irrational. And I see now that one reason for this was the fact that I was operating so far outside my comfort zone that it would be a four-day trek to get back to it again, and though the power of my monotropic fascination with making music was capable of pushing me way beyond my normal limits, there were still limits, and I was reaching them regularly.

And it wasn't just the gigs. There is much more to playing music in a band than turning up to play it live to people clutching pints. In many ways, despite the initial stress of getting on stage and the endless unfocused anxiety, playing live had a good, set structure to it that eventually brought a lot of comfort. I would turn up at the venue, unpack my equipment and plug it all together, take part in a sound check (the mechanics of which I never understood – I just repeated 'one-two' a lot like they do in the movies) and then sit and drink a few beers whilst waiting to go on. It wasn't easy, but it was predictable and strangely reassuring. I could handle this.

But practices, song-writing and marketing were all very uncomfortable at times. We were never able to commit to a single practice space, so ended up using three or four of them all scattered around Lincolnshire. They were all very different, with differing acoustics, equipment, journey times and (most importantly) personnel. One space springs to mind where the proprietor of an admittedly very nicely decked-out practice room on a pleasant farm was a very intense woman who took inordinate interest in our doings and kept offering us drinks. As I was always operating on the very cusp of meltdown during these times, the addition of such a person created a very fraught atmosphere and, looking back, I am surprised I never got as far as having an actual breakdown. Any kind of forced socializing when close to my limit can be very hard to handle. I can feel my mask – that artefact first created at primary school to handle social expectations – start to slip and fall away.

Usually, the first hint I get that this is happening is an inability to smile, despite knowing that I really ought to for fear of standing out in some way. So perhaps the extra person, the person whose presence has pushed me to the brink, makes a joke or something. Everyone laughs politely but I find myself unable to even grin. I know this will be noticed and commented upon, and as we know, that isn't something I can tolerate. So I busy myself with something so they don't see my granite facial expression.

If the situation persists, it's likely I will cease to be able to hide it and I can become quite overtly hostile (in a low-key, quiet way), perhaps snappy in my responses or actively scowling. Any further than this and meltdown is likely. Luckily it never got that bad, but it came close a few times.

About a year or so into establishing the band proper, a relative of a vague acquaintance of ours wanted to help us record a set of acoustic songs. He had some decent recording equipment, so we went along with it. This was a mistake. The fellow was inordinately intense, even mercurial, and had no issue with placing himself square in a position of authority. I never liked him, mostly because I didn't trust him and felt somehow that he was, to use the expression of my parents' generation, 'all mouth and no trousers' – meaning all talk, no action. I spent the whole time with him – and it must have been a few months of regular sessions – on the verge of completely losing my cool in a way I have never experienced since.

This is when the shield that a Special Interest provides can begin to break down. It had served me well, and would later begin to do so again, but my interactions with this individual smashed it completely. It is endlessly fascinating to me how for so many autistic people it is the presence of other humans that causes the biggest problems, and this was definitely the case here. My brain, already pushed to the limit by simply being in a band, was tipped over the edge by this one extra variable putting my precious routines and safeguards out of kilter. I'm certain that whole experience killed my interest in creating music – at least partly. It's interestingly related to a common phenomenon that autistic people often deal with. Go online to any autistic forum and mention how it feels to be joined by an unexpected third party when socializing with a friend, and the response will be a unanimous shriek of both recognition and fear. We prepare our minds for one thing – a process that takes a long time and a lot of energy – only to be winded by a curveball in human form. My experience with this irritating sound engineer was just a more intensive example of this, I believe.

❖

A year or so after that fraught recording experience, in 2008, we got the opportunity to play a gig at a fairly cool, underground kind of place in North London, somewhere near Archway. Considering the majority of our gigs to this point had been in provincial places like Skegness, Lincoln and Leicester, it was a great opportunity to showcase our tunes and try to impress the savvy capital with our country charms (we had begun billing ourselves as 'nature punk', where the nature was everything and the punk was a bit of an optimistic describer).

On the journey down I found myself increasingly fixated on the problem of parking. London is notoriously bad for this, providing far fewer spots to place cars than space on the road to drive them. I am never entirely sure what people are meant to do, other than avoid the capital at all costs, and the fact we had several thousand pounds' worth of equipment to haul from the car to the venue made my anxiety even worse. My brain considered every possible disastrous permutation of the situation. Perhaps we would get lucky, find a spot near the pub and then find ourselves getting towed away for some unknowable parking malfeasance. Maybe we would have to park somewhere in Elephant and Castle and take our drum kit three miles on the Underground. At absolute best we would end up exhausted, possibly bleeding and bruised, and crying; or at least that is how my brain weighed up the probable consequences.

As such, I could not engage with the light-hearted chatter of my bandmates on the drive down. My responses were terse and cold, as if backed by an unspeakable fury at the fact my bandmates did not seem concerned about parking in the slightest. I was aware I was missing out on those golden moments of being on the road, shooting the shit – the times you are meant to look back on as an elderly, dying man and wistfully, fondly recall – by being so preoccupied, but somehow that just made it worse. My brain was operating on the belief that if *we* do not worry about it, then who will?

As it happened, and as it had happened many times before in smaller cities around the UK, we found a reasonably good parking spot, down a side street about a hundred yards from the venue. But still my brain wasn't happy. There was still the possibility of being towed or assaulted by some overzealous traffic warden, and after all, I had not even considered the possibility of the car breaking down as we tried to leave. Shuffling that novel, exciting fear into its filing system, marked 'extra things you hadn't considered going wrong', my brain seemed to sigh in perverse contentment at a job well done, and I spent the rest of the day and night in a state of near panic, which considering I was meant to be singing on stage pretty soon, was not ideal.

We were playing last, in what was misleadingly billed the 'headline slot'. That meant sitting through four or five other sets, four or five other soundchecks, four or five other scurrying chaotic moments where equipment was swapped around. These bands were good. Local. They had fans that had packed into the dark basement, all holding bottles of Budweiser, dressed in tight jeans and shirts (this being the era of The Strokes and Kings of Leon). These fans loved the music, danced away, crowded the stage – it was a proper gig, filled with energy and life. After a few bottles of beer my anxiety about the car exploding when we turned the ignition began to fade; not disappear – no amount of beer could make that happen – but become more manageable. I began to look forward to playing our music in front of this committed crowd of obvious music fans: how fun it would be to sing the Forest Song at them, to hear their applause when we finished one of our noto-riously short and extremely loud songs.

When the last local band finished their set, the place emptied. It was just us – the four members of the band – and a few friends and well-wishers. In my memory someone even turned the lights on, but I may be misremembering that. But I am certain that we played to an audience of perhaps four people that night, excluding ourselves.

We can take a moment here to consider something known as 'rejection sensitivity dysphoria' (RSD), which is an interesting 'feature' of some neurodivergences, with autis-tic and ADHD people reporting it as a trait they experience.

Still in its infancy in terms of research and understanding, and existing in that peculiar limbo where there is a considerable amount of scepticism and doubt that it even exists (see dyslexia in the 1990s), RSD is a debilitating condition whereby any kind of emotional rejection, whether real or imagined, has an enormous impact on the wellbeing and mental health of the individual, far outstripping the impact a neurotypical person would feel. It is damaging enough when the rejection is an irrational, ungrounded fear – such as an autistic person being absolutely terrified they have offended or upset a friend when they do not get a WhatsApp reply immediately – but when the rejection is real and abundantly obvious, the effects can be extremely serious. Fears spiral out of control, self-confidence collapses and anxiety spikes horribly, and playing to an essentially empty room had this predictable effect on me. But do you imagine this was my first time? I was 25 years old – of course it wasn't. I had been here so many times that I had a wardrobe packed with the t-shirts. A seasoned old master of these involuntary crushing meltdowns, I did what I did best: hid it from everybody around me.

We played the whole set, me shouting out the lyrics in an unusually harsh and brutal fashion (which must have been quite an experience, considering the lyrics were generally to do with farm animals and walks along quiet country pathways) and the rest of the band putting in a fantastic performance. It may well have been our very best gig – certainly better than Oxford, where I was described by a cruel yet fair BBC reporter as being akin to a less harmonious Shane MacGowan – and was definitely a high point of our musical careers. The nervous energy I had bottled up all day was bursting out as a kind of musical meltdown, which is an experience I had never had before, nor have I had since. Usually meltdowns are pretty destructive: sometimes physically, sometimes emotionally, but this one was at least channelled into something decent, the explosive and chaotic energy dissipated through the strings of my guitar and the fragile cords in my larynx. Afterwards, exhausted by a day of terror, I slumped as everyone drank some beers and we got packed up ready for the long drive back up to Lincolnshire. Photographs were taken, but I only know this thanks to the digital artefacts themselves; I have absolutely no memory of them happening. The drive north must have taken a few hours, even that late at night, but other than a vague memory of sliding into bed at the very end of it feeling absolutely dreadful, I have no recollection of that either.

I was clearly running at the very limit of what I was capable of, and it was the Special Interest, the monotropic obsession with music and its creation that allowed me to overclock myself so much for so long. I had spent perhaps five years pushing and pushing, doing things that were so out of my comfort zone they might as well have been radioactive, and this gig and all it entailed seemed to crystallize that bottled-up stress.

It was the last gig we ever played as a collective. Soon after my friend, the co-founder of the band, moved to South-East Asia, I began my teaching career and that was the end of Sires of Nothing. Music has continued to occupy me from time to time, and I even had a brief stint in a covers band as a lead guitarist in Bristol for a few years (nothing would induce me to try my hand at singing again), but it never regained that same primacy over all else. There is a reason this chapter falls in the middle of this book, and that is – unlike every other interest described in it – my Hyper-fixation on music ended as abruptly and confusingly as it began; whilst all the rest of my obsessions over the years have waxed and waned but ultimately stayed intact and accessible, my total love of making music died completely. I have not written song lyrics in over ten years; I haven't formed a new melody to a set of words for nearly 14 years. Sometimes, Hyperfixations simply die.

And as for my taste in listening to others' music, as I approach 40 I am increasingly comfortable with allowing myself to be led by whim and fancy; I no longer feel the pressure to 'get it right' in some strange way, and those times where I still get to settle down and listen to music (for example whilst writing these words), I have gravitated most to a nostalgia for the days I mentioned in Chapter One: eighties songs by bands such as the Eurythmics, Pet Shop Boys and Erasure; the music of my mum and dad. I suppose now that I do not expend the energy or time in music as I did when it was my primary fixation, I have fallen back on the tried and trusted, and as I have no intention of starting a retro electro revival any time soon, I am freed from the enormous pressure of listening to music that would in some way improve my own compositions. Finally, after 20 years, I can relax into music like it's a lovely, warm bath and just... luxuriate in it for a time.

And I still don't know who my favourite band is, either.

CHAPTER FIVE

War Games

Ah, *Warhammer 40,000*, or '40k' as it is affectionately known by its many fans. A game so exceedingly expensive that it would genuinely be much cheaper to buy a decent second-hand car than a fully equipped and painted army of models, but, goodness me, as if that would ever stop us collecting them.

The premise of these 'tabletop war games', as they are known, is simple – both players field an army of miniature figures, ideally painted and carefully sculptured to make them both beautiful and unique, and they set about fighting using a comprehensive set of rules, tape measures and a bucket full of dice. It is fundamentally a numbers game. Every miniature has an accompanying line of statistics that determine how likely they are to accurately shoot or strongly bash their opponent, how tough they are, how impenetrable their armour is and so on. Every engagement becomes a series of dice rolls, making the game feel at times like an extremely complex version of Yahtzee, blended with poker. And it is fun – an awful lot of fun. Typically, games will be played in shared spaces (as the playing 'board' of this game is usually a six feet by four feet slab of wood, it makes sense to have a lot of these set up in a big room, like a church hall or community centre of some kind), which means your fight will have onlookers, there will be tea or coffee or beer in abundance, and music may be playing in the background: it can be a party atmosphere all round.

For such a widespread hobby (there are 500 dedicated shops around the world, from the UK to East Asia, and the company made sales of £361 million in 2020 during the Covid lockdown), it is still viewed as an extremely niche one, populated by geeks and weirdos, and as you can imagine, is fairly heavily associated in the public eye with young autistic boys. The image is one you'll often see at secondary schools across the UK – a small boy, maybe 11 or 12, lugging around a huge moulded black plastic box bigger than his own torso to an after-school club, typically in the school library. On opening the huge case, a myriad of half-painted models will spill onto the table and the games will begin. Well, might begin. It depends if the combatants get past their discussions of rules, models, the extensive lore and extraneous details. Often the game may make a faltering start after perhaps 45 minutes of this… other times it may not begin at all, though both parties will depart having had a thoroughly good time!

Certainly, in my experience as a teacher, the students who attended Warhammer Club were almost exclusively male and often had a diagnosis of autism. In some way, the hobby seems tailor-made to suit the various aspects of autism that autistic boys frequently present: obsession with details, statistics, in-universe lore and stories, miniature worlds and model-making. As a result of this, it is a highly gendered hobby, and though there are a growing number of women hobbyists, they are still vastly outnumbered by the male.

❖

I spent the years 1997–2001 attending an all-boys school in Spalding, Lincolnshire. This is smack in the middle of the Lincolnshire Fens, an area of flat farmland that radiates out around the estuary of the Wash between Boston in Lincolnshire and Hunstanton in Norfolk. The town is an ancient, sleepy market town and farming hub, once famous for its tulip parade every spring, now more famous as a place for the elderly to retire to enjoy the pleasant climate and relatively quiet streets, and to indulge in their favourite pastime of voting for the Tories. Being part of Lincolnshire, the town had somehow, like much of the rest of the county, managed to retain its selective state school system of grammars and secondary moderns, which had been phased out across the rest of the UK in the 1970s.

As such, when my family moved here from Leicestershire, I was forced to sit a test to gain entry to the prestigious Spalding Grammar School, which had been established in 1588 by some friend of Elizabeth I. On a summer day we drove across the country so I could sit this test, alone in what I think was the head teacher's office, with three bits of work in front of me: an English test, a maths test and a bit of French writing (who I was, my favourite place to go, my height, eye colour, hair colour and birthday, of course). It was a very strange experience, having grown up in a county that didn't separate kids out based on an arbitrary score on a single test, but I'd been told that the alternative school, should I fail, was so scary and horrible that I had little choice but to pass.

Thankfully I did, and my time at this strangely posh, yet totally publicly funded all-boys establishment began. By this point in life, I was already interested in Warhammer, having been bought a few boxes of plastic warriors the year before, but I felt intensely intimidated by the all-male culture of the school, a male culture that wasn't ok with the idea of painting miniatures and playing with them, but instead was very masculine, sporting, and cold. My interest in Warhammer scurried underground, into the shadows: a secret shame.

Because although it is a very male hobby, tabletop wargaming is not universally accepted by all men. Male culture, in the UK at least, is strictly hierarchical in nature and the irony is that despite autism being stereotyped as a 'male condition' and famous autism researcher Simon Baron-Cohen's insistence late last century that autism represented the 'extreme male brain', as if it was everything that encapsulates masculinity wrapped up in one befuddled skull, autistic men are about as welcome in masculine circles as a cat in a washing machine. If you were to take a stereotypical autistic male, with their Hyperfixations and their social insecurity, and place them in the midst of a group of confident neurotypical cishet men, then it would be reasonable to expect that bullying, or at the very least mean-spirited bantering, would occur within minutes. Or, even worse, they could be completely ignored or shunned, treated with such contempt that they barely warrant being looked at.

And so, in schools and workplaces across the country – across the globe – we can find little enclaves of autistic men as a kind of sub-stratum to what is generally established as 'male society'. It is a familiar enough trope from the media, after all. Think Maurice Moss in *The IT Crowd*, whose lack of social skills and esoteric interests make him either vulnerable or invisible to other men, or Martin Prince in *The Simpsons* – you know, the short orange-haired child in Lisa's class who dances around in orange shorts and white shirt, spouting information like an encyclopaedia. These are characters that I found solace in as a child, recognizing them as related to me in some way, but for the majority of society they are humorous figures to be mocked and ridiculed, usually by neurotypical guys, amused by their social ineptitude.

And so, we hide ourselves away at school, in libraries, little-used classrooms, round the corner in the playground where everyone forgets to go. We huddle and we talk and we play Warhammer with the few other individuals who understand us. This is how it was for me. I actually had a kind of split in my small number of friends between those who knew of and shared my hobby and those who did not, and a vivid memory of mine was when the truth emerged, some time in Year 11. It was always going to happen – the two friends were in the same class, for goodness' sake – and the fact I thought I'd get away with it speaks to immense naivety on my part. My Warhammer buddy had brought some stuff into school and during break-time eagerly asked my opinion of it, whilst I sat with my other friend. My options were to fess up or enter into some kind of elaborate pantomime of confusion and denial.

I seriously contemplated the pantomime of confusion and denial.

The fact is I knew all too well what the consequences of this would be. I had absorbed through the years a clear understanding that my true self – who I really was behind the mask I had been constructing since nursery school – was liable to bullying and ostracizing, despite being autistic and therefore 'struggling to understand social cues'. Believe me, some social cues are beaten into you deeply. The summer before this moment had been that final family holiday with my grandad that I mentioned in Chapter Two. I was fully obsessed with Warhammer and all I wanted to do was talk about it, and in doing so succeeded to alienate pretty much everyone there with my talk of Dark Elves, magic phases and painting techniques. And this was *family*. I had absolutely no chance with people lacking a blood connection.

I fessed up. It was met by immediate derision along the lines of 'You're not into *that* shit are you?' and the friendship was never the same afterwards. We drifted apart pretty quickly and by the time we were studying for our A levels, we were no longer friends. The effect of this was that I had to fully commit to the small group of Warhammer fans (I believe there were probably five or six of us), and from that point on my desperate attempt to at least remain palatable to the rest of my peers evaporated.

As wonderful as our Special Interests or Hyperfixations

are, you see, there is always this risk that they will alienate us from people, that the target of our intense interests is somehow so deeply 'uncool' that even associating with them risks being cast out and ignored. The fascinating thing is that some subjects of this kind of monotropism, held perhaps by neurotypical people, are seen as entirely acceptable and even encouraged. The amount of detailed knowledge that football fans have in the UK, for example, or baseball fans in the United States, verges on the extreme and can definitely compete with the most obsessive of Warhammer fans, and yet not a peep of complaint. Being fixated on these sports or games is viewed as understandable, a rich part of our culture, and allows access to many other masculine groups and pastimes.

I don't think the unfairness of this systematic behaviour is lost on autistic people at all – like me in my form room, caught between two friends, we have all had to make that choice between leaning into our interests without shame or hesitancy, and fighting it and keeping them hidden or at bay to try to remain acceptable to the neurotypical majority. It is usually an impossible fight that few end up winning. I fought. I'm not sure I won.

✤

Upon moving to university, as you saw in Chapter Four, I managed to take on music as a new interest and my love of my painted miniatures was forced into a small box, both physically in the attic back home with my parents, and emotionally in a tiny corner of my brain. I was terrified of being unacceptable to the people at university, scared to death that I would fail to make friends there or end up some kind of social pariah. Most of all, I was desperate to finally and belatedly enter the arena of romantic relationships, and I saw my little soldiers as an absolute barrier to achieving this. Apart from the occasional surreptitious glance through issues of *White Dwarf* (the magazine associated with the hobby) in the newsagents of the student union (when I was certain that Charlotte behind the counter wasn't looking), I squashed that interest flat for years. My miniatures gathered dust in my parents' attic but were never truly forgotten – I have found in my life it is impossible to truly destroy a Hyperfixation; even music didn't die completely.

It would be five years before I dipped my toes back in. It had to happen, of course, but the mechanism by which it occurred is an interesting one. The only reason I ever allowed myself back into the fold was that my friends in the band – Tom and our short-term bassist, long-term friend Andy – were both allowing themselves to be immersed into it too. I remember it vividly. We were particularly drawn to the *Lord of the Rings* licensed game made by the same company as *Warhammer*. This was 2006 so the fervour that the movies whipped up was still strong, and the miniatures were of great quality. On one fateful road trip to nearby Peterborough, home to a Games Workshop store, we all chipped in to buy a copy of the game. After the irrelevant but noteworthy distraction of watching a tornado gusting across the flatlands on our way back to Spalding, we set the game up on my parents' dining room table. It was like sliding back into a warm bath after being interrupted by a knock at the door.

The game box was filled with models representing the Orcs of the evil Dark Lord Sauron and the soldiers of the city of Minas Tirith. Of course, they were unpainted, and our first job was to clip them into their little round bases so they would stand, but even in this rudimentary state, fighting and manoeuvring between salt cellars, mugs and other hasty 'landscaping' on an old wooden table, the scene was impressive and the game was extremely good fun. I was hooked once again, this time feeling far freer to truly enjoy the hobby without that irritating feeling of embarrassment: I suppose I was finally growing up, growing into myself properly.

For it is a terrible thing to be ashamed of your Special Interest. I would hope, by now, I have made it very clear that these interests are extremely important to the wellbeing of an autistic individual – they are absolutely vital, and trying to indulge them in secret, out of the way, separate from large swathes of the population, is a painful situation to be in. I am lucky that apart from the hobby outlined in this chapter, most of my others have been perfectly palatable for the general populace (though it was admittedly touch-and-go with LEGO® for a while, and a few folk view my obsession with the *Titanic* as a little strange), but I do have some other interests that are very important to me that I hesitate to announce in a freely available book, for fear of being seen as callous or unpleasant or morbid in some way (my interest in disasters, both natural and man-made, does not end with the *Titanic* – Chapter Eight's focus – and includes some disasters that are recent enough and political enough to be viewed as such), and other autistic folks may have similar problems.

But the difference between hiding a geeky interest in school and gradually leaning into it openly in adulthood must be a frequent thing for many of us. I have a tremendous amount of respect for any school student who manages to wear their nerdiness on their sleeve, and have been known to defend them when necessary. I have seen this from my adult, teacher perspective many times. One student, many years ago, was extremely interested in trains to the point they would carry around a model train to lessons and talk about them to anyone at all who would listen. They were viewed as peculiar but were so confident in their interest and their sincere desire to share that they somehow managed to transcend the possibility of bullying.

Another, more recently, was a huge fan of 90s video games, rather like me. They carried around several plush toys in lessons, and a sketch book where they would draw characters from the video game series whenever they felt stressed or overwhelmed in class. They were always absolutely bursting with information and facts about the latest developments in the fandom (most of which flew over my head, with my acquaintance with the subject ending in around 1998) and again, were fairly indiscriminate in who they aimed this data at. But things for this student didn't go quite so well, and I would often have to support them when they were punished for retaliating against the relentless bullying they faced.

One time, I heard they had received a detention for pushing a student over on the playing fields to the rear of the school. I was told by a senior teacher, who was recounting it in a world-weary fashion, as if imploring us to empathize with the difficulty of dealing with such a terrible child as this. I asked what their reason for the pushing and shoving was. 'Oh, you know that bloody silly toy [they] carry around everywhere? One of the lads had nicked it and run off with it.'

'I see. So, what punishment is the other lad receiving?'

'Nothing, he didn't push anyone.'

I have rarely been so furious in the workplace. I made it very clear, I think, how unreasonable this state of affairs was, and demanded that our Sonic-loving friend have their detention revoked and for the case to be set up as one of bullying, rather than a one-off altercation. With reluctance, this went ahead, but the sour taste left in my mouth after this would take many years to fade. In fact, I'm not entirely sure it has faded. The problem is, there aren't enough autistic teachers to go around protecting all the autistic students: non-autistic teachers have to pick up that slack and protect them too. I wish they had done this for me and my friends back in the late 1990s.

⬍

Back in 2006 I was happily immersing myself in the hobby once more. In fact, I was allowing myself to swim around in it, explore the nooks and crannies. I soon widened my interest beyond the *Lord of the Rings* game and back into *Warhammer Fantasy Battle* and *Warhammer 40k*. And why not? As I had grown past the capacity for shame it seemed only natural to enjoy the full hobby.

The range of models had improved a lot in my five years of absence, and had also gotten slightly cheaper, which is something of a novelty in itself. Back in the 80s and 90s the majority of models were made of a lead-based alloy, which was easy to mould but also not particularly hard or long-lasting. In the mid-90s more basic models came moulded in plastic, but the technology was young and the capacity for minute detail on these models was limited. This was the era of boxes of eight identical plastic models, which even when painted looked a little strange and false on the battlefield. Higher-value models, representing heroes or wizards or generals, were by this point in time formed from an alloy known as 'white metal', a replacement for the soft and toxic lead. But this was expensive. As such, my army of Dark Elves in the late 90s didn't look great – metal models cost more than I could afford and plastic ones looked, quite frankly, crap.

But by 2006 they had somehow developed the technology to create intricately detailed models out of a new, tougher plastic. The difference was amazing to behold. The new plastic enabled sets of models to be adaptable and customizable, so each basic model would look different and have a unique pose. Even unpainted, a fully assembled collection of these new miniatures was a brilliant sight; painted, they were truly beautiful. And to top it off, these new plastic sets were considerably cheaper than the metal. I filled my boots. I am not ashamed to say that by the time I was earning my first wage as a teacher, I was building up a huge collection of little soldiers and finding the time to paint them.

I continued with *Warhammer Fantasy* where I had left off – collecting the evil and ludicrously twisted Dark Elf faction. These are a strange mish-mash of Viking legend crossed with old Marvel comics. They were a dark and spiky bunch, painted in lots of golds and blacks and purples and navy blues. The best indication of the kind of vibe Games Workshop was trying to achieve with them is the fact that their cavalry ride Velociraptors rather than horses and their most dangerous unit is a horde of scantily clad female elves welding huge machetes. They are the Scandinavian heavy metal of the wargaming world.

For my foray into the sci-fi *Warhammer 40k*, I decided to go for their spiritual opposite – the Eldar. These are essentially space elves, taking cultural cues from the elves of Tolkien and the mechanized war machines of *Gundam* (though not as much as the obviously anime-inspired Tau faction). The idea is that they were a proud and noble race that were brought down by their own hubris and debauchery – a sort of galactic Fall of the Roman Empire but with more robots. They are a group of aliens brought to the brink of extinction, with a different way of viewing the universe. Now I know I am autistic I can begin to see why they drew me in so strongly.

I ended up with a good-sized army for both factions, and was so absorbed in the hobby that I remember spending a trip I took to Aberystwyth on the far side of Wales with my then girlfriend plotting and designing army lists and working out how to use them, rather than being present at all in the moment, apart from a brief period where I stood agog at the fact there was a Frisbee Golf course on a cliff top above the town (I guess the town isn't fond of its university student demographic at all). As is always the case with me, at its height this interest took up perhaps 80 per cent of my brain's focus at any given time, and I would often drift off to sleep imagining different colour schemes for my warlocks who rode around on magic flying bicycles. I even had the opportunity to play the game more at this point, in comparison to my school days. A friend I had made during my teacher training course (possibly the only true friend I made in the period 2005–2019, at which point my Twitter activity led to several firm friendships) was a big fan of the game and we would drive up to Lincoln every Thursday evening to play games in a vast church hall just down the hill from the cathedral.

At the time I was living in a small market town called Sleaford, just on the edge of the Lincolnshire Fens, about 25 miles away from my parents' home in Spalding, and as quiet and boring a place as you could imagine. It would be five years before the town's name was placed firmly on the musical map of the UK, with the rise of the electro-punk duo Sleaford Mods (who have little to do with the place and chose the name mostly thanks to both growing up fairly nearby). I was teaching in a girls' grammar school in nearby Boston in my first proper job and I was reasonably happy. I was living with my partner at the time, two cats (the enormously characterful Dylan and Dawn – sisters in only genes) and a snake called Stewie. And I had a new friend, enough little soldiers to occupy me for years and a Warhammer club for regular games, filled with a wide array of interesting folks, only a 40-minute drive away. It was the final months of my band days, as outlined in the previous chapter. Everything was reasonably settled and calm, and it's a period of my life I look back at with some fondness.

So, as you can see, a quiet, happy and calm period of my life directly coincided with my acceptance and full immersion in interests that I had forced myself to deny for a long, long time. I do not see this as a coincidence – it is clear cause and effect. Allowing myself to be me, tearing off the mask (or at least that part of the mask that hid my geeky interests) that I'd worn for too long, had done my mental health the world of good. If I had been able to settle into myself earlier, at school (and damn the haters), then I feel I would have had a more contented time between the ages of 15 and 25.

It's all very good to speculate, but to return to a major theme of this chapter, it's much easier said than done as the fear of bullying, othering and being ostracized is hugely influential in those teenage years, especially for an autistic person, and *especially* especially for an autistic person who is undiagnosed and desperate to be seen as 'normal'. If I could have my time again, even knowing what I know now about my brain, I can't say with absolute certainty that I would fight that judgement and be myself: the impact of bullying is just too much.

Our favourite deepest interests are not always benign helpers, even if they have that capability. Often, they are dangerous in that they will set us apart, flag up how different we are to the people around us, and encourage those people to find ways to hurt us and belittle us. I couldn't write this book without acknowledging this darker side, and to remind everyone reading it that there will be thousands of autistic people – especially school-age children – who face bullying on a daily basis for the 'crime' of being fascinated by a subject that does not appear on the predefined list of topics that are cool (as I've mentioned, football is on here, baseball in the States; TV shows like *Love Island* feature too, as might celebrity culture generally). These autistic students require moral support and encouragement to lean into their interests, and their mocking peers require education.

Ultimately it is a ridiculous situation, and quite damaging, and not least because tabletop games like Warhammer are so useful as an analogy to how the real world works for an autistic person. This may sound silly – after all, how often do you find yourself throwing frag grenades at orks when in Sainsbury's? – but the regimented structure of how the game operates, plus the randomness factored in by the use of dice, is probably the most instructive metaphor for getting through life as an autistic person that I have come across.

Let me explain. As I have touched on briefly before – necessarily, as I'm all too aware how easy it is to lose an audience when discussing this topic, so I have carefully lulled you into being more receptive to this – a game of

Warhammer involves taking turns, just like a conversation or reciprocal relationship. One person takes their turn, the other person reacts, and so forth. And before all of this we have the 'deployment' phase, where each army is placed on the board in tactical, strategic ways.

In so many ways this echoes how I approach socializing and occasions and the like. I prepare myself fully, and assume the other party is doing exactly the same thing. Before I join an event, be it something big and grand like a wedding (and how I could, if I had the space, write an entire chapter just on that topic) or rather more small scale, like meeting a friend for coffee, I will mentally prepare for it in minute detail. At the very least I will trace my steps and progress through the event in my mind, and if it's possible to physically do this by visiting the venue in advance, you'd better believe I will do it. I will even go so far as to open Google Maps (possibly my favourite invention of the 21st century to date) and have a good old peer around Street View to figure out the lie of the land. Neurotypical readers may be nodding away to this, having done similar before extremely high-stakes moments like job interviews. Good for you! But I do it for everything, including before grabbing a latte with a friend I've known for years.

All of this preparation feels so similar to the careful placement of units on a battlefield. Like that, it is all about prediction and erasure of bad variables – removing chances for things to go horribly wrong. I put my squad of heavy fighters right *here* so that my opponent's heavy armoured vehicles can't go this way and will likely end up going over *there*, where I have created a great ambush point by putting these two squads of fast troops *here* and *here*. All of this is trying to set out to control what happens, to be able to rest easy knowing what is likely to unfold. As an autistic person this is how I live my life, with my regimented routines and practice runs all designed to eradicate any chance of things going wrong, which in my world is code for 'not going as I'd hoped'.

Once all is prepared and in place, then I suppose I am begrudgingly ready to attempt to handle the engagement. In a game of Warhammer, this is managed with the use of a tape measure and a huge pile of 6-sided dice, or d6 as we tend to call them (this is to differentiate them from all of the many, many different sized dice that exist out there in Geekworld, from the satisfyingly pointy d4 to the vast and vital-to-playing-Dungeons-and-Dragons d20). We use the tape measure carefully, minutely move our miniatures around the battlefield in moves so precise that it can take up to 20 minutes just to move the units fielded by one side. Obstacles are avoided, cover is taken, hills are climbed and vehicles boarded.

Once this is complete, then the killing begins! Or at least shots are taken, and probably missed. Every unit wielding a 'ranged weapon', usually a laser gun of some kind but occasionally a very imaginative tool that maybe squirts lava or something, gets to try to hit an enemy. This is achieved by throwing all the dice (I'm serious – it's not unheard of to have to throw 20 to 30 dice in one go) and seeing how many achieve a score high enough. The standard is getting a four or more (so 50 per cent), but this can be modified by a host of factors such as the miniatures' skill level, the range, use of cover and much more. After the dust has cleared (well, dice) then you remove as many miniatures as you have managed to horribly maim with your squirted lava. And the game continues.

This combination of intensely careful manoeuvring and random outcomes is so familiar to me as an autistic adult that I am beginning to believe they could remarket the entire game of Warhammer as the 'Autistic Social Life' game. I choose every single interaction and utterance with tremendous care, especially if I have the time and freedom that social media provides. I plot each conversation in advance, just as a tabletop game fanatic might spend their time before a game working on strategy and movements on the board. After so many years of social interactions I have a pretty good idea of how people are likely to respond to my words – this is a necessary consequence of all that mask building and etiquette learning I outlined in Chapter One – and as such I can pre-empt possible pitfalls, carefully pick a path through thorny issues and shield myself from a barrage of criticism.

Let's break it down a little: after all, it happens so quickly it's impossible to follow in real time. I shall take an example that I recall very vividly – one where I was teaching a student in school who was very skittish. Some students are like that – like deer who will flee at the first opportunity – and you must tread very carefully to gain their trust. I have a piece of writing that the student must do, mostly for assessment but also because it will really help their self-confidence to get it done. I know that if

I mention assessment, or grading, or even hint at me ever reading their work, I will lose them and the 'game' is over. So, I choose my words carefully. I weigh up every single one against how it has been responded to in the past, as best as I can. I know that I cannot appeal to their work ethic because they are all too aware how artificial and arbitrary schoolwork is – they won't fall for that old chestnut. So, I slowly deploy my argument.

'It'd be interesting for you to see if you understand that bit of the play, wouldn't it?' I ask nonchalantly. 'I remember always getting confused about those two characters and it bothered me so much.' Good start. Laid down the initial line there, avoiding the trap of school-speak and 'work for work's sake'. 'I reckon you'll surprise yourself with how well you get this play, you know.' This strategy has worked in the past with this student – they are pretty good at English and enjoy the reading side of things, the stories, the consequences and so on. 'Often writing it down from your own head really fixes your understanding of them, I find.'

By this point they were starting to respond. Well, they had picked up their pen. So far so good. But there is a randomness about human interaction that can skew the best-laid plans of mice and men – the dice rolls that can determine the outcome so cruelly. 'Maybe you could try to see if you could manage to write down to maybe...' I point at the paper, about half-way down, 'maybe down to here?'

With a clatter the dice show their results. All ones and twos. Failure. The pen is dropped again, and the student begins to close up – the gamble of referring so baldly to the physical act of writing was a bad idea, a scuffed target. But, as in a game of Warhammer, there are more turns. More attempts to get it right. I take a different tack, trying out a newer, less tested strategy. 'I bet once you start thinking about it you'll realize the hidden, secret link between these characters.'

Bingo. On target. This has spurred their curiosity. The pen is picked up and the student looks up and starts asking questions. They end up writing a good few paragraphs about the characters in question. A success, in the end.

Anyone reading this will no doubt be thinking how this isn't that dissimilar to their own experiences, but to them I say that this is the norm, not an unusual outlier. For me every exchange, with every person, in every situation is played out like this, having to judge every word, carefully plot my way through and deal with the catastrophe of random reactions. Many autistic people, driven so strongly by routine and the predictable, want this to spread into our social experience too – a world where we can always predict how people will react, how they will respond. Not through any desire to be all-powerful or controlling, but out of the same drive that dictates our love of routine generally: an exhaustion with the world where anything unexpected is just one extra source of exhaustion.

But of course, there is absolutely no avoiding the random nature of interaction, just like you cannot remove the dice rolls from a game of Warhammer. It is inevitable, and as such you work very hard to compensate for it. In the game you have contingency plans, careful placing of units, back-ups. In conversations you have equivalents: stock phrases to be deployed whenever things get confusing, back-up topics of discussion, carefully planned openings.

It is interesting to me how much of life I have managed to rationalize by viewing it through the lens of gaming. As I discussed in Chapter Three, much of my social life has been handled as if I were a character on *The Sims*, and as I have just described I cannot have a conversation with anyone without being reminded of a game of Warhammer. The fact is, gaming of any kind is a controllable, managed and, most importantly, safe space. When you sit down to a game of Monopoly you know what the limits of the game are, you know the aim and you understand the mechanics. Well, mostly – Monopoly may not be the best example given how many local variations of the rules exist! (A shout-out here to everyone who places fines and other miscellaneous expenses in the centre of the board to be collected by whatever lucky individual lands on 'Free Parking!')

For a demographic of people for whom the world is always threatening to spin wildly out of control at any moment, 'gamefying' your existence is a very tempting strategy. After all, nothing truly bad can happen in a game. If you lose a game of Scrabble no one attacks you. If you mess up at Cluedo, you're not about to get arrested for impersonating a police officer. If Dizzy Dizzy Dinosaur (look it up...) goes wrong, no one dies.

I have managed to make peace with much of my life in this way. I have even viewed writing this very book as a kind of game, treating it much the same as any long-term 'grind' and awarding myself when milestones are reached.

Anything that involves self-help or development I view like a combination of a video game's experience points and a tabletop game's strategy and progress – if I go for a long walk, I imagine my stamina stats increasing as they would on a role-playing game (RPG). If I get the washing up done, I view the rest of the kitchen as being like a big board game: one sector is down but now I need to move to neutralize the gas hobs and then take down the region around the bin. It's an automatic thing, and it helps me so much in my endless quest to Make Life Easier.

It would be foolish of me to devote an entire chapter of a book to the autistic joy of tabletop wargames without spending a bit of time talking about the process of painting the miniatures. It is an unusual feature of autism that some physical activities are often essentially impossible and therefore out of bounds – it's so common for throwing and catching to be a real problem, for example – whilst others are mastered and accomplished with relative ease. I spent my childhood cowering during PE lessons, hoping against hope that I wouldn't be asked to take part in anything competitive. The few times I was made to take part, I would immediately and irrecoverably foul up to such an enormous extent that I would never be asked to partake by that teacher again. As poisoned chalices go, this is a doozy: you get what you want (i.e., a reprieve from having to take part) but it costs whatever tiny amount of social capital you may have managed to save up amongst your peers.

The memory of seeing your attempt to throw a ball at a teammate, only for said ball to slingshot vertically, high into the air, landing about a foot away from its starting position, lingers for a long time.

But when it came to the micro-movements needed to carefully paint details such as gemstones, eyes, runes and such onto miniatures only an inch tall, using a paintbrush so fine it might as well just start calling itself an eyelash, I was in heaven. It didn't come immediately to me, of course. For a while my miniatures were daubed in thick coats of bright shiny silver and gold, the equivalent of a young child's crayon picture. But before long I was able to correctly build up the fine layers of detail required to make these models look truly impressive. A base coat of black paint, slightly granular for texture, with layer after layer of carefully drybrushed colour (the art of scraping a brush with only a tiny amount of paint in order to leave pigment on raised surfaces, leaving the creases and pits in darker shadow), building up to more vivid hues. Time spent adding the little details, trim and facial features (should the model *have* a face, of course) and it was done! Only 99 more to go.

The fine motor control required to do this is pretty impressive. Completing that final stage of detailing requires a very steady hand and tiny little movements of the hand and fingers, and yet I could manage it easily – at least compared to more macro movements like throwing, catching, kicking a ball. It's like my hand and fingers are perfectly capable of doing complex things (remember, I'm a guitarist too), whereas my arms, legs and torso are completely hopeless, incapable of coordinating themselves at all. It reflects aspects of my personality generally – I'm great with fine detail when planning, writing, thinking, drawing but much less confident with big-picture stuff, and I wonder if there's something linking the two.

I would probably conclude that there was if it weren't for the existence of dyspraxia. Unlike dyslexia, which is a widely known condition, dyspraxia is fairly obscure. Like its 'dys-' cousins, Lexia and Calculia, it describes a set of issues operating within a certain frame: in this case, body movement. It is common to see autistic people who are also dyspraxic. It describes a kind of chronic clumsiness but goes way beyond that. In fact, it covers all kinds of difficulties with physical coordination, from being bad at sports to not being able to trust one's own proprioception (that sense we have that informs us of the location of our limbs, even with our eyes closed). It even covers an over-lapping issue with executive function, which seems to be affected by pretty much every neurology going, including autism and ADHD. I do not have a diagnosis of dyspraxia, and if I'm honest I don't think I would thanks to my decent ability with fine motor movements, but my absolute hope-lessness with macro movements may well, in some way, be related to my being autistic. And there is always and forever the possibility that my fine motor control isn't as good as I think it is, that in fact I have had to practise way more than others might have had to for the same results. The difference would be I never had a Hyperfixation on anything sporting or full-body, whereas I did, of course, with finer movements.

In any case, the world of Warhammer will probably always be a favourite for some autistic children, in that it scratches so many itches we tend to have. Whether it will ever be more acceptable to the general school population is another issue, of course. But at least I was able to enjoy it in adulthood. For, of course, autism is for life – not just for childhood.

◆ CHAPTER SIX ◆

Building My World

People spend a lot of time and energy talking about autism in childhood. This is a good thing, of course – after all, autistic children can have an absolutely awful time at school, at home, out and about, and the more we try to improve things for them the better. However, it has led to the enduring idea that autism is a childhood condition, rather like chicken pox or head lice. This is unhelpful on two levels. One, autism is not a disease nor some terrible scourge that can be removed with the application of drugs or some kind of folk treatment. It is a difference in brain structure; one is born with it, one lives with it, one dies with it. Two, as I have just alluded to, autism persists into adulthood and beyond. There are, in fact, far more autistic adults alive right now than there will be autistic children, due to simple demographics; many of them – most, perhaps – will lack a diagnosis, but this does not take away from the fact they are autistic adults, trying to continue to make sense of a world that continues to be very ill-accommodating. Autistic adults are real, they are here and one of them has written this book.

I have touched already on how adulthood is often a challenge to a great number of autistic people, and how

I have certainly found it to be rather tricky. But what is it about that transition that causes the biggest problems for us? For me it's simple: expectations.

In my experience, being autistic is a lifetime of shattering people's expectations, and not in that exciting, proud 'winning the Olympics despite what my PE teacher said about me' way. More in a 'Oh, you thought I was capable but oh boy have you ever screwed up employing *me*' way. My life is a long series of people being immediately impressed when they first interact with me, and then that hugely positive opening gradually eroding away as I fling disappointment after disappointment at them. The only real question is – for how long can I maintain the positivity?

For a very long time, I believed quite reasonably that this was a terrible character flaw. Even though I had no idea what caused this collapse in standing, I assumed it must be entirely my fault and therefore solvable in some way. The reality is, of course, that I was running way over capacity the whole time, pushing myself to do things that my nascent autism and chronic conditions made inherently more difficult, my self-flagellation over my perceived laziness making the situation five times worse as I insisted to myself that I must do these things that were, in fact, causing me great distress.

By the time I reached my mid-twenties I was in a job that, much like my band experience, didn't really suit my personality type. I had entered teaching as a way to try to secure better pay and conditions, and to make better use of my degree. At the time there was a shortage of

English teachers and the government were offering a decent grant to train, so I dropped my temporary job in a first aid training start-up in Lincoln and went back to university. My father was a teacher at the time. He had started late, getting his degree when I was a child, and he entered teaching in his forties, so I felt I had some experience in what the job involved, and an ear to bend when I needed to vent about the horrifying stress of the job. But the problem is that teaching is an extremely sociable job that requires an awful lot of time spent with other human beings, and as an autistic person I found this extraordinarily tiring. But of course, I did not know why, and so I bullied myself into persevering with it. The fact that I dreaded every single lesson, that I fought panic attacks as the kids came through the classroom door, were simply weaknesses I had to battle. So I did, and managed (to my credit, I suppose) to find ways to make this manageable – I found leaning into my Special Interests was the best way.

Talking to the kids about LEGO®, about video games, music and more got me through those years of teaching. I had LEGO® in my classroom – often building some set or another at break or lunchtime as a way to manage my anxiety, and I had long chats about video games such as *Red Dead Redemption*, *Sonic the Hedgehog* and *Grand Theft Auto* with my students during quiet times. It helped, but came with a certain amount of guilt that I was wasting valuable teaching time. I existed in a state of constant, debilitating stress that started to affect my mental health in a way nothing had managed to before. My defences, built firmly on my hobbies, were beginning to collapse.

Meanwhile, in Sweden, a young programmer known to the world as 'Notch' (real name Markus Persson, famous now for being an extremely problematic individual with very regressive views) had developed a new proto-game based roughly on the little-known *Infiniminer* where a fully formed three-dimensional world built of one-metre-cubed blocks was yours to mess around in, removing blocks here, placing them there, allowing players to create tremendously intricate and beautiful constructs with ease. Notch christened the new game *Minecraft*®, and an absolute behemoth was born. Between 2011 and 2014 you couldn't possibly exist in the Western world without hearing about this game, and even now, ten years since its official release, the game is going strong and has proven itself to be the biggest video game hit since the original *Super Mario Bros.*

I first heard about the game, like so many new and exciting things, through the students at school. All of a sudden, their creative writing was filled with details about building enclosures for sheep and finding pumpkins to make light sources out of. They all seemed to know what obsidian was, all of a sudden, and had a great interest in growing wheat. Assuming they hadn't all gone in for arable farming *en masse*, I realized they all had a shared experience through a video game, and that this was something I hadn't seen before: such a wholesale take-up of a new thing. It became a new topic of discussion in class, where I found out all about the best sources of gold and diamond, how to access alternative dimensions, and terrifying creatures called 'endermen', who would only attack you if you looked at their eyes, like odd reverse T-Rexes from *Jurassic Park*. It was obvious that I had to try out this game.

Downloading it in 2011 took moments and I was soon immersed. Having no idea what I was doing gave that first experience of the game a real edge, as it felt like I had truly been dumped in an alien world and left to survive. There were no instructions, no tutorial level or any explanation of anything, really. All one could do was experiment. It took me perhaps 20 minutes to realize I could harvest wood from punching trees, and a further hour to understand how to turn that wood into tools and, later, a home. But by this point I was hopelessly, irretrievably hooked. Here was something I could handle – here was a world where I could run away from the impossibility of handling adulthood as an autistic person.

I was obviously drowning in the energy requirement that masking and working in such a public-facing role demanded, and at the time I was without any of the interests I have outlined so far. The band was finished, had been for three years or so, and my interest in continuing to make music had collapsed. I owned no LEGO® at this time, all my childhood collection still in a box at my parents' house (don't worry – it's safe with me now), and I had sworn off video games at the request of my girlfriend at the time who, interestingly, had seen how reliant on them I was but drawn entirely the wrong conclusion from that. So other than time spent at work between lessons looking at pictures of steam trains I was completely bereft and without any of my usual activities. The discovery of *Minecraft*® came at precisely this moment and... well, I don't believe it to be hyperbole to say it saved my life at that time. Certainly, it pushed back my inevitable burnout (I'm a strong believer that, for autistic adults, burnout will come sooner or later) for at least five years or so.

As you know, thanks to my reminiscences in Chapter Three, I have immersed myself in video games many times, and have always found them soothing, but this game was something else entirely. I have to be careful not to gush too heartily here: I know I'm very lucky to have the opportunity to talk at such length about my interests but I'm acutely aware that I am completely capable of boring the life out of you if I start to go into detail about why *Minecraft®* is so good, so I will attempt to limit myself. Here goes...

When you start a new 'world' in the game, you can be sure that no one else has ever experienced the same place. The world is generated randomly, following a set of algorithms that determine the appearance of mountains, caves, oceans, rivers and the like. So, unlike a game like *Grand Theft Auto* or *Skyrim*, there is no game map that has been minutely crafted by the game studio as your playground. Instead, you have an almost infinite (seriously – a *Minecraft®* world is much, *much*, bigger than the surface area of Earth) randomly generated clean slate to work with. This makes your world your own. It becomes, over the coming weeks of play, your very own second home with all the preciousness that implies. And as second homes go, it is excellent. There is freedom to do whatever you like in this world of yours. If you wish you can dig down into the ground and carve yourself out a lovely underground lair, complete with caverns of farmed vegetables lit by artificial suns. Or you could build a huge tower, with a view high above the clouds, with a sophisticated mini-railway to ascend and descend.

Much like in real life, you begin with nothing but your own guile and desire to survive. In those early days this vast, unknown world you have been dropped into is a threatening place, filled with weird-looking critters that emerge after dark to groan at you and beat you up. Without tools, you are reduced to punching tree trunks to extract the wood required to start developing technology (a little less like real life – you could punch an oak tree for days and the only result would be bloody knuckles and broken fingers). Once you have a few planks of timber you're away, transforming this into rudimentary tools like pickaxes, regular axes, swords and hoes (agriculture is a surprisingly big part of the game: after all, you need to eat to survive), all allowing further exploration. You dig down and find coal, iron ore, copper, gold, diamonds – all of these materials can be used to further your adventure – but also echoing caverns packed with beasties like the ever-present zombies, skittering spiders and odd green exploding fellows who look disarmingly like dildos.

For many years the game lacked the traditional structure that most gamers are familiar with. There were no levels, no final boss, no end credits as a reward for your hard work. It just *was*, and it persisted forever until you got bored. These were the glory days in my opinion. The way this echoed real life was tremendously appealing to me and I loved the subversion inherent in this. It meant

I felt no pressure (unlike in every single other game in existence) and no imperative to tire myself out trying to 'solve' the game. For someone seeking absolute sanctuary from the horrors of reality, this was lovely. I would just mooch around, digging and building (or indeed mining and crafting) to my heart's content without feeling like the game's designers were breathing down my neck and trying to cajole me into situations to force narrative progress. Anything you can imagine can be built and enjoyed, and for someone who is finding real life increasingly frightening, this second home becomes a bolthole, a panic room – a safe space to go and inhabit when things are rough, as they almost always were.

At this point in 2012, life was too much to bear. I was living in a new city and was in a relationship that was doing neither of us involved any good whatsoever. Work was a pitiless parade of difficult lesson after difficult lesson and I suppose part of my brain just *snapped*. I view the short bout of depression that followed – the first in my life – as a kind of foreshadowing of what was to come later, a growling, menacing tremor before the volcano erupts. I took a week off work on doctor's orders and booted up the game.

Starting another new world I took in my surroundings – a wide open grassland dotted with occasional oak trees – and began to make myself a home. I had grand designs this time – I was going to try something new on this playthrough. I decided to construct a huge, fortified Norman-style keep with thick walls and secure, snug little rooms. It was a triumph of design. The walls were three blocks thick, which enabled me to incorporate the staircase into them, winding through the external walls. It had three floors, each with its own clear purpose, and a basement where I kept all of my supplies. In that week off work, my brain bubbling with unhappiness and stress, this castle was more my home than my actual bricks-and-mortar apartment.

It is interesting that my instinct was to build a castle keep, as it speaks volumes about my overwhelming feeling of being besieged by the adult world at this time. Clearly a part of my brain had determined that I needed some kind of metaphysical fortress to protect myself in while I worked through the nightmare I was living through. Interestingly, this careful establishment of a safe, impressive and well-designed bolthole in a virtual world was not reflected in reality – at least not at this point. My actual home was not a safe space due to the relationship issues that were occurring at the time (themselves a result of undiagnosed autism and mental health problems) and work was obviously veering on the side of dangerous in terms of the effect it was having on me. So, all my need for safety and security was poured into this video game, and every waking moment where I could inhabit it, I did.

I find this extension in the role of a Hyperfixation fascinating. I've already established how Special Interests in themselves are emotional safe spaces where energy can be restored, calmness established and peace found, but in this instance the interest became a much more blatant metaphor for this, and *Minecraft*® has generally continued to fulfil this purpose for me to this day. Many autistic people report having fictional, make-believe worlds in their heads to retreat into when they need it. A very good friend of mine tells me that her mental safe space is invaluable to her and is so developed and sophisticated that it has actual characters, locations and stories – all to allow a high-quality refuge when the going gets tough which, unfortunately, it so often does. It will come as no surprise to learn that she is a novelist.

Time passed. I recovered, life and relationships changed and then, in 2015, I became a father for the first time. This is where adulthood really smacked me in the head: everything up to this point had been shenanigans in contrast to the absolute, all-consuming terror of being entirely responsible at all times for another human life. We had spent so long preparing for the day, making sure we were completely ready for the huge change in life that would occur, but it was nowhere near enough. The moment my daughter was born, as amazing and affirming a point as that was, and as grateful I am to have her wonderful self in my life, everything changed in a way that my autistic brain was going to find extremely difficult.

On top of this, despite finding my job inherently difficult and stressful – enough to need to have a computerized escape hatch through which I could dash when required – I had managed to get myself promoted into a middle management role at the exact same time I began the adventure of parenthood. If you recall, I mentioned earlier in this chapter that adulthood for me (before diagnosis) was a series of moments whereby I convinced myself I was a terrible, lazy person and had to push ever harder to try to break through these awful personal flaws. I fear to this day that the double hit of extra responsibility at work and parenthood was a kind of natural progression of this philosophy – an inevitable result of feeling so strongly that my weaknesses could be strong-armed away with enough will. As you can probably guess, I was not able to meet the challenge.

Luckily, I had spent a few years leading to this point continuing to develop that one *Minecraft®* world with the big, strong castle home. After finishing this individual fortified symbol of why the game was so important to me, I had gone on to develop that empty place – just hills, trees, rivers – into a living, breathing country. I had built a city around my fortress of over a hundred buildings, with a high stone wall around the whole thing, complete with ornate gatehouse and towers. I built a second city on a stretch of coastline. A third city in the mountains. Innumerable castles, towers and ruins scattered across the map. Villages, all named, all populated, all busy with interesting things to find. Farmland, harbours, ships, temples and hidden caves – years and years of effort into creating my own, highly personal world. This was the tradition of autistic psychological world-building actually made reality – or at least something approaching reality – and it gave me a place to escape to that was not confining and claustrophobic but wide open, vast, free and growing all the time. I built my original fortress in 2012, around the time of the London Olympics, and I added a new village to the map just last week in the summer of 2021. In 2015, when I needed it most, it was already huge and sprawling enough for me to find some calm simply walking around it, enjoying the fruits of my long hours' work.

And so, the awesome challenge of raising a child was aided by a video game. I don't think I feel great about that, but I cannot avoid it. Autistic parenthood is a topic that gets ignored so frequently, by so many, that I feel it is almost my duty to explore it in greater detail here while I have the chance. I suppose it is all part of the continuing myth that autism is a childhood condition, that means the very idea of an autistic person having a child is viewed as odd or tremendously unlikely, but it is not. Over the last three years I have gotten to know hundreds of autistic parents, many of whose diagnoses were received after, and as a result of, their child's diagnosis. This is especially true for mothers, who were so much more likely to get through school without anyone noticing they were autistic thanks to the system's curious blind spot in that area when it comes to girls and their often greater capability for masking compared to their male peers.

There are thousands of autistic parents in the UK alone, and there is no support of any kind offered to us. Parenthood in Western society is actually, if you stop to consider it from an outsider's perspective, very scripted and socially rigid. In the UK, for example, we have the expectation of joining an NCT class (the National Childbirth Trust – a charity dedicated to educating new parents) that is so deeply engrained that before I experienced it directly, I had assumed it was a government service offered for free that we literally *had* to attend. I blanched when I found out we had to pay for the damned things. We have the social expectation of the 'school gates' – a phenomenon that is so tightly wound into the tapestry of parenthood that as noun phrases go it covers pretty much everything – the social groups and outcasts among parents, the gossip that inevitably occurs, the conflicts and arguments, as well as the physical actual brick and steel gateposts and gate of the school.

Parenthood is a series of very strong expectations and missing them can cause anxiety like nothing else can. From the labour ward to the school parents' evening, kids' birthday parties, swimming club and doctor visits there are rules that all must follow, or fear the terror of being shunned. This is not ideal for autistic people who struggle with all unwritten rules at all times – if they're so important, maybe we should write them down? – and I would imagine that the 'shunning rates', if there are such a thing (and I think there ought to be – it'd be fascinating analysis), are extremely high in the autistic parent population.

It is easy to see why and how: an autistic parent picking their child up from school is likely to be much quieter than their neurotypical peers, far more likely to avoid conversation or socializing and, if we do get involved, much more likely to screw up the interaction in some way, by making an ill-advised joke or similar (I have personal experience of this). Because children are children, and parents' protective instincts are on high alert in any of these situations, any sense of 'the other' is likely to cause immediate repercussions. There's not really any room for error.

Also, looking after a young child is something that

requires as much informal support as possible from those around you – not just grandparents and close family, but acquaintances, friends, colleagues and more, and the reality is that autistic parents lose access to a lot of this as a natural result of their disability: for much of our lives the way we tend to alienate (unwillingly) those around us really begins to hurt us. Our typically small, tight-knit friendship groups are not big or robust enough to truly help in those difficult days following birth, when post-partum depression may have hit and relationships are tested.

The social aspect of parenting, then, is problematic for autistic people. But then there's the practical side too. As a huge fan of closely held routine, I found the chaos and unpredictability of the first year or so more difficult than anything I had previously encountered. Babies are completely unattached to schedules, regard planning with disdain and are unimpressed by bedtime. Anything resembling routine you may have fought to build up over the years to help manage your extreme stress levels is suddenly thrown into absolute disarray, exacerbated by lack of sleep and general, ill-defined worry about the little urchin that is the source of all of your new woes. It is a common theme of this book so far that anxiety is an autistic way of life, that worry and overwhelming fear are a constant in our lives, and that our Hyperfixations help mitigate this to an extent: well, what happens when the stress is amplified but the opportunity to indulge in our interests is stripped from us?

I remember scrolling through some gaming forums

on Reddit, I believe – almost certainly one night when I had managed to get my daughter to sleep on my chest, but was now too afraid to move her – when I stumbled on a thread of folk talking about how they had adapted their video-gaming practice to the challenges of parenthood. This was probably 2016, so my daughter was around a year old and consuming, in her cute and generally adorable (if a little smelly and noisy) way, every waking moment of my life that I wasn't driving myself into an early grave at work. As such I trawled this thread with great interest. I had lately had no time to inhabit my fantasy world. *Minecraft*® sat, a dormant shortcut on my desktop screen, mocking me whenever I had to go online to check what the symptoms of measles or typhoid or bubonic plague were (with a new child it's hard to avoid some paranoia). In fact, I had no time for any of my interests at this point, and I was reduced to briefly reading content on my phone to get a slight hit whenever I got the chance.

The thread about gaming under the influence of having a baby to care for was an eye-opener. 'Just put them in a sling and game to your heart's content' was one optimistic idea. We had a baby sling, but the idea of sitting playing *Grand Theft Auto* with an infant swivelling her head to peer at the carnage didn't sit easily with me, nor indeed would I be able to sit easily with a sling anyway – they are uncomfortable at the best of times and even more so sitting down. Another suggested waiting until baby was asleep, which was so touchingly naive I felt I wanted to ruffle the writer's hair and wink at them. From my experience, babies *didn't* sleep – that was their whole thing. A third confidently asserted that the best way to game while parenting was to get your partner to take the baby off your hands so you could run around in a colourful fantasy world collecting trinkets or stars or coins or whatever.

I laughed hollowly. Imagine trying to broach that conversation. The fact was, my situation was completely out of sync with being able to spend time on things that relaxed me; so, like a dormant volcano slowly collecting a nice, pressurised bolus of magma within itself, I gradually approached disaster. My *Minecraft*® world was left alone, unplayed, unused and bereft, while my stress levels began to peak.

❖

Talk to an autistic adult for long enough and it's likely they'll mention 'burnout'. As abstract nouns go it's pretty commonplace and used by all kinds of people, of all neurotypes, typically to describe a point of utter exhaustion, usually within a workplace or other activity. People talk of their careers causing them to burn out, leaving them with no interest in that job and a dangerous lack of motivation. Within the autistic lexicon it holds a similar meaning but with one key difference: it's not a loss of interest in a job – it's a complete collapse of interest in living. This is not to say it is always accompanied by suicidal feelings – it doesn't work that way. More, it's a destruction of all motivation that seems to stretch, like a nasty haze of unpleasantness, into all aspects of an autistic person's life. Interest in our Hyperfixations vanishes, often *en masse*, leaving us completely vulnerable to the stresses that always threaten to overwhelm us. Interest in our friends and family can disappear in a similar way to how depression can affect people.

Possibly the most insidious thing about it is the way it strips you of your ability to mask, to pretend, and to fit in with the rest of society. All of a sudden, your autistic traits are out in the open, worn on your sleeve, totally exposed like a nerve with no hope of being able to sufficiently sustain any kind of defence. It is this moment – Autistic Burnout (and goodness me it deserves the capital letters) – that can ruin our careers, our relationships, our lives.

It was inevitable, looking back with my current knowledge, that Burnout would hit me sooner or later. As an accomplished masker with no idea I was neurodivergent, my endless self-flagellation for my self-perceived flaws guaranteed it. It seems to hit autistic people at different ages, though mid-thirties is a pretty common moment. For me it was when I was 33, a year into parenthood. Suddenly, and without any warning that I was able to recognize, my interest in the world around me collapsed, as did my ability to function. First to suffer was my job. As head of department, I was always intensely busy and disorganized but always somehow managed to get through, even excel at times. Now I was just helpless, surrounded by enormous stress and completely incapable of climbing on top of my workload and getting it under control. I began taking time off, heading home early, crying at my desk. It was noticed. Meetings were had, conversations shared. I took time off again – this time several months, long-term sick. I didn't really have a choice. I knew something had broken, though I didn't know what, and I was self-reflective enough to know I had little chance of piecing it back together again any time soon. I left school a broken man and didn't go back for eight weeks.

The trouble was that time at home wasn't exactly a balm to me. I had thrown in the towel with my job but still had the stress, worry and tension of parenthood. At this point, as depression crashed down upon me as an extra layer of horror atop my Burnout, I was struggling to do the basics, such as cook dinner, maintain hygiene, brush my teeth (I was to pay for this in time – depression can really screw things up long term). All the Special Interests in the world couldn't help me now – I was beyond their reach and had never felt further away from the safety and cosiness of my online fictional world. Instead, I threw myself into nature, going on long walks in the Cotswolds, taking photographs of butterflies and landscapes to try to cleanse my brain a little. For once the real world was a slightly more soothing place, up to a point. The removal of the layer of stress and worry that work provided gave me time to reflect and calm my brain. It also gave me time to pursue a suspicion that had taken root – that there was something fundamentally different about my brain and how I processed everything. I had read Mark Haddon's *The Curious Incident of the Dog in the Night-Time* many years earlier, so I had a pretty flawed idea of what autism was, but I knew enough to recognize that my love of routine and difficulty with social interaction fit quite well with what I had seen in my autistic students at school.

Reading up on the subject was difficult as there were very clearly two different tracks of thought and opinion. On one side we had the professionals – psychiatrists, professors, psychologists, all of whom took a very negative and pathologized view of autism. This didn't seem to fit with my experience – after all, I had been to university, had a job, a child. I'd been in a rock band for goodness' sake. None of this fit with the accounts provided by these doctors, who seemed to view autistic people as highly dysfunctional and unable to have anything approaching a normal life. They also focused entirely (or so it seemed) on children. I was 33, long out of school, and therefore seemed to be irrelevant to their interests. It was all about school and teachers and academic difficulties and so on – nothing about paying council tax, arranging doctor's appointments for your child or managing employee/employer relationships.

Luckily, there was the other track – this was populated by actually autistic adults who were surprisingly happy to share their experiences online, on forums such as Reddit, Facebook and, of course, Twitter. These gave a much more balanced and useful account of autism – one which chimed so strongly with my own experience that I remember being absolutely staggered by it. They spoke of parenthood, of Special Interests, of relationship hardships, of problems remembering to do vital stuff – they were describing my life.

I stormed to my GP's office and demanded an

opportunity to get a diagnosis. Well, rather I meekly mumbled my reasons to them as they stared at their computer screen. But within a month I had an appointment with a psychiatrist and the rest, as the cliché goes, is history. Once my diagnosis process was under way, I poured energy into sharing my experience online. I had about 3000 followers on Twitter at that point, gained from a decade of writing intermittently about the woes of the British education system, and was eager to add my voice to those exceedingly useful and friendly autistic adults who had helped me figure myself out. After perhaps six months I had got the official diagnosis letter, following three extremely traumatic long sessions with a psychiatrist asking me for details about my entire life up to that point. I now knew why I found life so difficult, I knew much more about how my brain worked and (I hoped) had a chance to heal and sort myself out.

I remember that week of getting diagnosed I had a moment of free time and opened up *Minecraft®* once more. It had been perhaps a year, but my world was still there, waiting patiently for me. I wandered around the kingdoms, cities, villages with a happier, more at peace soul, revelling in the creativity I had poured into this virtual haven over the last five years. Something had snapped into place in my life and though there was still a long way to go, for the first time in years, looking out over the beautiful, blocky, pixelated landscape of the game, I felt hope.

❖

I often wonder whether my experience of *Minecraft*® is shared by the autistic community at large. Certainly, it's a very popular game amongst that demographic, though I don't know whether that is for the same reasons as I have. But it is a very autistic-friendly game and has been since the very beginning. Its similarity to LEGO® is obvious, in that you can construct whatever you wish from blocks, and so all of the reasons for the Danish toy's popularity that I explored in Chapter One are relevant here too, but it goes beyond that. One of the things that made *Minecraft*® so immediately attractive to me as a LEGO® fan was the fact that, yes, it gives you the ability to build great structures, but it also gives you the landscape to build it on. Unless you are some millionaire with a LEGO®-filled basement, it is very difficult to amass enough LEGO® bricks to construct a few roadways, let alone hills, forests, beaches and mountains. The few people on Earth who do have this option are lucky, of course, but unless I do *very* well out of this book I cannot realistically hope to join their ranks (a single decent-size green baseplate can cost a few pounds, and you would need thousands of them). *Minecraft*® gives you a whole world to fill with your creations, and it is already there, ready to go – no assembly required. When I set about building something new on my erstwhile world – the one I hide in whenever I can – I always begin by scouting out a suitable location: a spot where my idea will take root and inhabit. Sometimes, the landscape itself gives me the idea. The point is, *Minecraft*® has much more scope than LEGO® ever could, and all for under £20.

It also scratches that ever-present itch to collect, as

Pokémon does, to go around finding things and gather them up. Every *Minecraft*®er worth their salt has a storage room that is their pride and joy: a vast space filled with wooden chests, each one neatly labelled and filled with a certain category of material that will undoubtedly be useful at some point in the future. As you go around the world, chopping down trees and mining underground, you fill your inventory (think huge pockets or a massive rucksack) with stuff, from rubble to dirt to leaves to iron ore to diamonds. Every single one of these materials has a potential purpose or utility, and so there is an absolute urge to store every single one carefully. Honestly, it talks to my autism like it speaks its language, and going around, organizing my wares, is one of the most relaxing things I can do (see also *Skyrim* and *Subnautica* for similar forays into inventory establishment).

On top of all of these excellent autistic-suitable features, we can add the logic the game works by. I don't wish to perpetuate the stereotype that all autistic people are logical to a fault, as plenty of us are not, but a large number are and this game suits that mindset very well indeed. Its internal rules are consistent and reasonable, and easy to memorize. Things are almost always as they should be within the world of the game: you can always find diamonds at a certain depth underground; farmed plants will always grow according to set parameters; rare creatures and structures will always appear on the map ('spawn') in certain identifiable spots and regions. It is no wonder the game acts as a calming factor for me: it feels at times as if it were purposefully designed with that aim in mind.

But the logic doesn't end at internal rules. The game has a huge sub-genre within itself – what is known as 'redstone' but is, in actual fact, basic electronics and programming.

Redstone is a mined substance that's pretty common and acts as a combination of energy source and energy transport: a kind of battery and wire in unison. You place it upon blocks in the usual way, but with careful manipulation can create in-game equivalents of anything that can also be made out of electronic equipment. So, for example, it is possible to build circuits, with lights, switches and so forth, but also (if you have the kind of understanding of electricity that I sadly lack) transistors, logic gates and even rudimentary memory. With sufficient application and a huge amount of knowledge it is possible to craft in-game calculators, even basic computers, out of this red material. This means you can enter a strange meta-world of having a computer program running within a computer program, which can give me a headache if I stop to think about it for long.

But as I'm sure you can appreciate, with the popularity of programming software like Scratch and easy-to-use introductory hardware such as the Raspberry Pi, this is the kind of thing that is hugely appealing to most teen-agers, and especially those with the capacity to get fully immersed and sink hours and hours into it. As autistic Special Interest focuses go, it is so deep and rich as to provide an unending source of fascination for years.

In short, it is a perfect interest.

I credit *Minecraft*® with a lot. Unlike most of my interests, I believe it saved my life, more than once. After

I reopened the game following my diagnosis, I continued to develop it – have continued to, in fact – and it grows and grows every year. That sprawling fictional world, entirely my creation, continues to be a kind of partner to me. I associate every part of it with a period of my life over the last ten years. Hell, I associate every part of it with the music I listened to as I built it. The mountains and tunnels, castles and monuments all have a story to tell. It is a biography in a language only I can understand, and walking around inside it is the closest I could get to reliving my life.

Occasionally I will boot up the game, enter my world and go to a particular spot – a mountain that I designed and modified several years ago. This is the part of the map that I was in the process of developing when I discovered that I was going to be a father, and in walking its paths and viewing its vistas I revisit that amazingly potent moment so vividly. I suppose any ten-year endeavour could harbour similar emotions and memories – perhaps writing a huge novel or building a boat – but there is something pure and simple in it instead being this childlike game within which I have built a literal world to explore and inhabit. It is my panic room, my sanctuary and my memory, all rolled into one.

Needless to say, I have this world saved in about seven different places. A few files in the Cloud, a couple of different hard drives and a memory stick. It is precious to me far in excess of any of my other 'stuff'. My LEGO® is valuable, and I love it to bits, but were it to be stolen, I would simply have to slowly buy it all again. My video games are precious but easily replaced. My guitars have history behind them, and I would be sad to lose them, but as physical artefacts could be re-purchased. But my *Minecraft®* world is utterly irreplaceable. Should I somehow lose every save file, like Voldemort losing his horcruxes, there would be no way to walk through those memories again, no means of recreating it all. Ten years of endeavour and memory locked up into a few gigabytes of data that I guard with everything I have.

So yes, when it comes to Special Interests there is a reason *Minecraft®* gets an entry separate to other video games. For it's not just a game to me. It is, quite literally, my life.

CHAPTER SEVEN

Heroes and Villains

Everything changed for me in 2016. I had flirted with political activism a tiny bit whilst a student in 2001 thanks to the invasion of Afghanistan (well, I bought a couple of Michael Moore books and felt angry all the time), but I had never pushed it very hard. I remember 1997 and its crowning moment of a Labour victory against the reviled, utterly ruined Conservative Party, rocked by endless scandal and sleaze, and I also recall the downfall of that particular government as the David Cameron Tory Party rose up in 2010 (this was a period of posting glum takes on Twitter), but it wasn't until 2016 that I became truly invested in the political scene.

Of course, it was Brexit that made this happen, and of course I was (and still am, in some small, shrunken way) a Remainer. I would imagine that will have become abundantly clear in the preceding chapters, though I may be wrong about that. But the referendum of 2016 became my world for a time – I was fixated by it, sensing that the result would affect every aspect of my life moving forward. It did, but I wonder how much of that effect is self-inflicted rather than a consequence of anything external. Certainly, the years between that summer referendum and the Covid pandemic of the early 2020s were dominated by politics for me. But that is not the subject of this chapter. In fact, despite my obvious obsession with politics at this time I would not go so far as to call it a Hyperfixation in the style of music, gaming or dinosaurs. It is as if my brain recognizes the cold, boring reality of global politics and replaced it in the grand scheme of my interests with a proxy – a bigger, even more consuming fascination with fictional heroes and villains.

After all, Doctor Octopus and Thanos are far more fun than Boris Johnson and Donald Trump, even if the latter are way more dangerous. My brain, pickled and packed with concepts to do with good and evil, right and wrong, fixated on a cinematic marvel that began in 2008, long before that summer of discontent, with the release of an ambitious film by the name of *Iron Man*. In 2008 (and it's very hard to remember just how different things were back then), the Marvel Comics character Tony Stark and his shiny red-and-gold alter-ego was actually fairly obscure. Certainly, he had none of the awesome clout of Spider-Man, whose star had never waned but had been significantly boosted by the success of Sam Raimi's movie trilogy earlier in the decade. Then you had the awesome might of the X-Men, whose absolutely seminal 1990s Saturday morning cartoon had led to a blistering flurry of movie hits from 2000 onward.

Iron Man, much like Captain America and Thor, were second runners to these truly big names, and tended only really to have fans within the world of comic books. At the time, it's very likely that Blade, the Fantastic Four and

Daredevil were more famous in the world of cinema than these fellows. And the movie industry knew it. *Iron Man* was a huge risk, funded heavily by John Favreau (who was desperate to get an Iron Man film out there at long last) and abetted by the clever comic-book guru Kevin Feige, who (it turned out) had absolutely huge ambitions for this particular movie. Feige had worked on the earlier X-Men movies and the Raimi Spider-Men and was known in the industry as highly knowledgeable and passionate about the source material, but back then I doubt anyone truly grasped what he was up to. Realizing that the comics' biggest draw was the vast shared universe, with characters popping up in each others' stories, Feige set about establishing the same idea, only in film. And so, the Marvel Cinematic Universe was born.

And my god if it didn't tickle pretty much every aspect of my autistic brain. I have always adored what we English Literature graduates call 'intertextuality' – the way different texts (and here I'm using it in its broad, academic sense which includes movies and television shows) refer to one another, bounce off each other and generally show awareness of each other's existence. As a kid I was deeply enamoured of the way that *Mork & Mindy*, the Robin Williams show about the fish-out-of-water alien making a life in Colorado, was a spin-off of *Happy Days*, and a little later, how *Frasier* had spun from the orbit of *Cheers*. It was all endlessly fascinating to me, as it made logical sense that fictional worlds would share a space. After all, the physical real world all occupies the same area – Venus and Colchester both exist in a shared universe – so why shouldn't TV shows and films? But for whatever reason, fictional spaces usually refuse to cohabit. Even those that did – like the aforementioned American sitcoms – never really leaned into their sharing of a space, and nine times out of ten it was never even mentioned.

The most irritating example of this, as far as teenage Pete was concerned, was the absolute refusal of both *The Simpsons* and *Futurama* to commit to co-existing. After all, it would be so simple! The latter show was based a thousand years into the future, making it easy to basically *be* the future of the Simpson universe. The characters were drawn in exactly the same style. The humour was almost identical. But it was years and years before the shows finally caved in and had a brief crossover (as I recall, Bender the robot from *Futurama* appeared for the briefest of moments before vanishing again).

I hated this. I wanted all my favourite shows to exist together, mostly because I wanted to see the characters and storylines interact. There are many reasons why autism and fandom overlap – especially fan fiction – and one of them is the sheer joy of imagining character interactions that do not exist yet. Typically, autistic members of a fandom (the term refers to the group of very dedicated fans that a fictional franchise might attract; big ones include *Doctor Who*, *Harry Potter* and *Thomas the Tank Engine*) are extremely devoted and know the subject inside out and back-to-front. They will have watched every moment multiple times, meaning the only way forward is to create their own stories using the pre-imagined cast of characters. This gives a fictional franchise an immortality that its original creator cannot hope to bestow, unless they are incredibly prolific. And needless to say, a common trope in fan fiction is 'crossovers', where characters emigrate between franchises.

It wasn't really until I saw the first *Avengers* movie in 2012 that I realized what Marvel were playing at. They had carefully introduced four characters in their own solo films – Iron Man, Captain America, Hulk and Thor – plus two as supporting characters in those films – Black Widow and Hawkeye – plus a villain in the form of the previous antagonist from *Thor*. Suddenly a movie was doing something I had always wanted – it was purposefully turning a series of movies, with big-name, established characters (and big-name, established actors), into something more akin to an extremely high budget TV series, with its long arcs and storylines. But it was also completely unafraid of letting these huge characters interact. Argue. Bicker. Joke around. At one point in the film, all of the would-be Avengers are arguing on board Samuel L. Jackson's flying boat, camera flitting from megastar to megastar, and I realized: my god, I'm truly watching a comic book.

The comics published by Marvel were never, ever squeamish about doing this, you see. They love it. Characters come and go all the time, crashing each other's tales and causing friction and friendships. Some, like Deadpool, are so fluid in their travelling to others' stories and worlds that they even break into our own, communicating with us directly, breaking the fourth wall, fully aware they are in a comic book. As media go, they are perfect for anyone who has that desire to see their favourites interact together. But it had always seemed folly to try to translate this onto the big screen, which is why it didn't happen until 2012.

Of course, once that dam had cracked it soon burst completely, and the Marvel Cinematic Universe blasts from strength to strength. My obsession with it really started to become worthy of inclusion in this book with 2016's *Captain America: Civil War*. This loose adaptation of a comic story arc of the same name was most notable because it included the introduction of a true, solid gold comic book character into this shared universe: the youthful, exuberant Peter Parker, or Spider-Man. Played as a proper teenage boy, with girl issues and a huge amount of LEGO®, this Spidey was very similar indeed to the comic version, and I was truly hooked. The idea of a film featuring properly developed (over the course of four or five earlier movies) versions of Iron Man and Captain America feuding whilst assisted by Spider-Man and Antman was just intoxicating. I couldn't believe it was happening, or indeed that it was even possible, and I went to see it in Bristol's Showcase Cinema on its first day of release. I wasn't disappointed, and thus began a truly intensive interest that has not abated to date.

One thing about these Hyperfixations we autistic people enjoy is how demanding they are of us. When I'm not actively exploring or indulging one of them, a small but extremely loud part of my brain is constantly whistling for attention, desperate for me to switch my attention from work, or my daughter, or making dinner, to whichever interest is currently ascendant. And of course, with media-based interests like this one in this chapter, there's only so much official content that you can watch. Once you've watched all of the films, multiple times, where do you go to satiate your enormous appetite for more information, more data, more detail?

Well, happily, there are plenty of other people out there who will share your interest, and even more happily there are some with the time and motivation to fill the Internet with everything you will ever need. I've already mentioned fan fiction – it alone could easily absorb even the most obsessive fan for a very long time indeed. Admittedly it is of varying quality, but it doesn't matter: it's out there, so if you wish to read a story where Thanos gets married to Captain Marvel you will probably be able to find it. And if not, you could always write it yourself. Then there are the wikis. Wikipedia is usually where people's experience of 'wikis' begins and ends, but it is only the tiniest tip of a vast iceberg. The word 'wiki' is one of the few Polynesian words in the English language, along with 'kahuna', 'taboo' and 'tattoo', and it means 'fast'. Hence an online wiki of any kind is a quick and efficient source of information, and there is a wiki for just about every possible text (again I use it in the academic sense) imaginable.

If you are obsessed with, say, *Thomas the Tank Engine* (which was inches away from being included as a chapter in this book) but you've finished watching all the TV episodes and films, then you can go to the Thomas wiki at Fandom.com and browse its *twelve thousand* pages, *one-hundred-and-forty-seven thousand* pictures and more. These figures are amazing but, for an autistic obsessive such as myself, completely unsurprising. Part of the experience is breaking down every tiny detail we have, analysing every mote of world building, characterization and storyline. The fact there are 10,000 discussions on that wiki is absolutely understandable, as far as I'm concerned. There's a lot to discuss in the world of *Thomas the Tank Engine*!

And if you get bored of that content (and believe me, for an autistic fan of the show it's bound to happen sooner or later), then you can mosey over to the second-biggest wiki out there – a website called TV Tropes. Started as a way of listing and categorizing recurring tropes (i.e., narrative devices) in the TV show *Buffy the Vampire Slayer*, TV Tropes is an absolutely vast site that seeks to categorize the tropes, devices, characters, and themes of every single media product that has ever existed. You can go on there, look up a trope (for example, the very common one of bad guys explaining their plans just before killing the protagonist, known as 'Just Between You and Me' on the site) and see every single book, game, play, film, show and musical that the trope has ever been employed in, plus a dash of interesting analysis. It is no exaggeration to say it is possible to lose hours upon hours to this website as you sink deeper and deeper into it.

And then if even that loses its fascination for you, you can resort to forums like Reddit and join in the never-ending churn of discussion and debate. I spend a lot of time on there, constantly checking the 'subreddit' (the name given to a community dedicated to a particular subject) given over to advance news and rumours about upcoming Marvel Cinematic Universe projects. As you can imagine, this is thanks to my finally having exhausted both the wiki and TV Tropes as sources of intriguing information. It was always going to happen.

❖

When I was eight or nine years old, I got punched in the face. It is the only time this has ever happened – I'm no fighter – and so it is fairly strongly bruised on my memory. It was after school, and I had gone down to the little brook nearby with a friend. I'm not entirely sure why. Sometimes there were frogs and newts down there, so perhaps I was on the traditional juvenile hunt for frogspawn. There was a group of other children down there – kids from my year who I knew vaguely, and mostly because they were a group of bullies who spent presumably 100 per cent of their time making others miserable. They were busy though, huddled down, backs to us, peering at the ground. I wandered over and saw they were watching a large frog in the stream. As they muttered, I could see its watchful eye flitting between them as it breathed very visibly: giving the impression of fear even if there were none.

Suddenly they moved as one, closing on the frog. They were obviously trying to catch it and, given their history, I doubt it was to do anything pleasant. As they rushed at it, I rushed too, shouting for them to leave it alone. The leader of the pack wheeled around and without *any* hesitation punched me very hard in the jaw. And I mean there was *zero* time spent thinking or considering the ramifications of such an act – I still think about it sometimes: the idea of having that act of violence as a first resort, a default. But anyway, it hurt a great deal (I was only eight and he hit like a truck), and I stumbled away in tears, shocked that such a thing could happen.

The frog was fine, by the way. I heard the next day that they were annoyed with me for letting it get away.

So why this anecdote? Contrary to what you might be thinking, it is not to imply Marvel-like heroism on my part (though I am glad the frog got away). More, it is to highlight an autistic trait that I haven't brought up yet – an absolute devotion to justice, which may lie behind my Marvel obsession.

It's possible that you have spent time online interacting with autistic people. After all, you may yourself be autistic. If you have, I would be very surprised if you hadn't noticed the amount of campaigning, advocacy, solidarity, and intolerance of intolerance that exists in the online community. It is absolutely everywhere. I just took time out to scroll through my Twitter feed (I'm dedicated to the most rigorous research, of course) to see what the lie of the land is today – early in September. Now, I follow upwards of 2000 autistic accounts on there (I would follow more but my feed gets overwhelming past a certain point) and so my scrolling gives me a decent idea of what's happening in the community today. And what a day it is.

There is a new research group out there, led mostly by non-autistic people, and they are being extremely disingenuous about how they interact with the adult autistic community. So, it's a Tuesday, as the meme goes.

Nothing particularly unusual about this. And as is always the case, the autistic community is rallying and organizing to challenge this unethical and (frankly) slightly dodgy organization. And it's incredible to see.

Some are organizing talks and discussions either on Twitter itself or outside of it. Others are putting together open letters for us to sign that communicate our unhappiness. Still others are directly emailing key figures in the research organization to complain. Generally, there is a strong sense of righteous anger at the whole debacle, but all of it seems to be being channelled and directed into action. And this is absolutely normal. Many people's first awareness of an autistic adult is likely to be Greta Thunberg, who became extremely famous extremely quickly in 2018 after refusing to attend school every Friday to raise awareness of the ongoing climate crisis, or *Skolstrejk för klimatet*. Since those early days, Thunberg has become an incredibly famous climate activist – possibly the most famous of all – and she is, of course, autistic. Now, I can't pretend to know any of Thunberg's motivations but I can certainly say I am unsurprised to see an autistic individual fighting so hard for such an important cause.

The fact is that autistic people seem to very frequently have an extremely strong sense of 'fair play' and justice. Maybe it stems from our apparent 'rigidity', in that we are unwilling to bend the rules (this is so often presented as a negative by neurotypicals that I can end up questioning their integrity, but that's another story). Perhaps it is rooted in some lack of susceptibility to what I scientifically christen 'bullshit' – there is certainly *some* evidence that fake news isn't quite as effective on us – or our close analysis of situations we find ourselves in. It is possible it is just a deep-seated part of being autistic that, thanks to its being a positive trait, has been completely ignored by researchers. Whatever the case, it is definitely a 'thing'.

As I mentioned at the beginning of the chapter, my experience of politics from 2016 onwards has been very difficult, and I wonder how much of this is caused by my autistic need for reasonable behaviour and fairness. As I mentioned at the start of the chapter, my political beliefs are pretty comprehensively progressive. They just are – that's how my brain works and I am not here to try to get you to feel the same way. It is no secret that for the last five years or so the chasm of understanding between what I suppose we would call the 'left' and the 'right' has grown and grown. Sometimes it feels like it is impossible to bridge it or manage to reach any kind of consensus at all, as we are all so vociferously opposing one another on almost every subject – education, defence, health, human rights, climate; it feels only a matter of time before the left and right pick sides on the 'pineapple on pizza' argument and make that the next battle of the culture wars.

I have watched it all unfold and throughout I have felt my strong need for fair play strained beyond its limit. It's the nonsensical lying, I think, that has caused me the most pain. Autistic people can lie, and do not trust anyone who argues we can't, but as a rule we see it as being unfair and unreasonable and can get extremely upset by it. The concept of lying is quite fascinating to me. I see the benefit of a 'white lie', for example. The kind where you're saving a person's feelings. I can understand why individuals might lie out of desperation or fear. That is something I can wrap my head around.

What I struggle with is cold, prepared lying. Perhaps as an offshoot of this need for justice, I tend to assume as a default position that everyone on Earth is essentially good and reasonable, and I still, at the age of 38 years old, feel surprised and hurt when it turns out not to be the case. As such, the absolute cheek of the barefaced lies that politicians have taken to telling (realizing, I fear, that the consequences are way less severe than they had expected, and running with it) has shocked me over and over again. How can such lying happen? It isn't by accident or in the heat of the moment, nor is it to spare someone's feelings. It is, quite simply, purposeful deception on a grand scale and it's no wonder my blood pressure has been around 180 over 100 this last half-decade. From the £350 million smeared on the side of that big red bus advertising the pros of Brexit, to Donald Trump claiming the 2020 elections in the United States were rigged in some way, the lies are huge and they pile up. And worse, they are rarely called out for what they are. Some arms of the media actively support them, using their vast weight to lend legitimacy to outright nonsense, whilst others seem too afraid to speak up and use the bluntest terminology to call it what it is – outright lies.

For me, an autistic individual standing by watching it unfold, it is absolutely unbearable. The injustice of lies being allowed to stand and percolate through the population, wreaking havoc as they go, is something that causes me actual pain. People pop up and make pithy observations that 'politicians have always lied' and such-like, without recognizing the huge, tectonic shift that has taken place. Sure, I remember the politicians of the 90s lying, evading questions and so on, but there was always a cost. Bill Clinton, lying about his adventures with Monica Lewinski, was impeached and – unlike Trump – actually came within an ace of being convicted. Tony Blair, lying about Iraq's possession of nuclear and biological weapons, had his legacy reduced to tatters and is now one of the most hated politicians around. There were resignations, heads hanging in shame at being caught out, and public apologies and more.

Nowadays, none of this appears to happen. Politicians lie brazenly, knowingly, on air and they stay in post. Politicians are caught doing the most horrendous things and they are fine. Even if they are sacked for their misdemeanours, like the UK's Priti Patel, they will only be re-appointed a little while later when the outrage has died down. On top of all of this, and this is where my blood truly begins to simmer, vast swathes of the voting public seem not only to accept, but to encourage it. It is a cliché to say that all autistic people seek logic in their lives but there's some truth behind it. Certainly, illogic and lack of good reason are viewed by most autistic people as Bad Things, and good cause to argue against – and these days that seems to be all that politics is: an endless parade of clear illogical cause and effect and a lack of sensible, honest judgement.

It is little wonder that I have sought refuge from this confusing and infuriating world in a universe where bad guys are dealt with, and the good guys maintain a clear sense of reason. Nobody in the Marvel films responded to Thanos' plan to destroy half of all life by partly agreeing with it and working out a weird compromise, or by trying to gaslight others into seeing its good sides. Nobody wrote an opinion piece saying, 'Well, let's consider both sides of the genocidal argument.' Instead, the heroes were unanimous in their feeling that it was not a particularly sensible idea, and that it might be best to try to stop it happening. It is my feeling that if Thanos were to arrive on Earth here and now, in 2021, he would be met with a decent number of people who would support him and go on the news to praise him for 'making the tough decisions' and 'saying it like it is'. And that is something that I struggle to cope with.

⟐

The pursuit of absolute fairness begins in an autistic person's early childhood. I remember it being in my life from the earliest times. Obviously, it fuelled my foolish endeavour to protect the frog – for the frog had done nothing wrong and was simply trying to get through its day – and it was the driving force behind any issues I had with teachers in classrooms. I could not bear injustice of that type. Children getting blamed for something they had not done was infuriating, and I would sit and rage quietly at how the teacher had let us all down in that instant. By the time I was at secondary school and more likely to encounter the horror of whole classes being punished for one child's crime (I don't know why this was so prevalent back then – was it actively taught to teachers during their training?), I was beginning to get the confidence to push back, though I was still far too shy to make a real go of it.

Instead, my best examples of this trait in action come from my time as a teacher, observing autistic students. As an autistic teacher I tried very hard – possibly way too hard, given how difficult it is – to be fair; I knew I had to, as nobody likes a hypocrite, and I knew I wouldn't be able to live with myself if I emulated the unreasonable teachers of my own school days. As such I was scrupulous. If a student misbehaved in my class, I would be utterly transparent about how they had messed up, making sure they understood in no uncertain terms what had gone wrong. This was important as I remembered how frequently fellow students would be left confused about why their teacher had singled them out or shouted at them.

Once they understood, I would then explain very clearly what the consequences already were, and how they would continue to grow should the misbehaviour continue. There was no room for error or ambiguity. All was ordered and clear, settled and obvious. I had one of the quietest and nicest classrooms in the school as a result of this, with students who knew where they stood and where the boundaries were.

But it wasn't always perfect.

I remember one time when a student in Year 11 was furious. They were in the corridor outside my classroom and looked to be very close to entering a severe meltdown. I knew they were autistic and, in fairness, they knew I was too, and so I tried to discern what had happened. The student was a frequent victim of bullying, but was also themselves something of a bully – a fascinating dichotomy built on a lack of confidence, as far as I could tell, and a feeling that the only way to be accepted was to be mean to others – and so it was often very tricky to identify what had actually happened. But this time, it seemed fairly clear. The student had been goaded over and over by one of their regular tormentors to the point that they had snapped, unable to control their frustration and rage any longer.

The snapping took the predictable form of a scuffle – a fairly bruising fight just outside the library that had continued upstairs into the path of a member of the school's senior leadership team. And this is where things went truly wrong. For whatever reason, it was the autistic student who was singled out by the assistant head. Perhaps it was prejudice, or just bad luck – it is impossible for me to say – but it was absolutely unreasonable. There is no question about it. To pin the blame for the scuffle on the victim of the initial verbal goading was not on, and so I felt the need to intervene. The student, though, was absolutely furious at the injustice. I knew exactly how they felt. It's a white hot, lumpen feeling in our torso, a feeling of pain and utter discomfort, visceral and instinctive. I could liken it to the feeling one gets when in imminent danger, when one knows that something truly disastrous is about to happen, only with added anger at a world content to allow this disaster to unfold.

They began shouting at the assistant head. Proper shouting too – the way only an angry 16-year-old can.

It reminded me of the scene in the Michael Douglas film *Falling Down*, where his character suddenly decides to hell with it and attacks with a baseball bat a couple of gangsters who threatened him. That dropping of all civility in the movie was taken as a sign the character had reached some threshold, some limit of what they could handle. The student had clearly experienced similar.

Of course, shouting at a senior teacher is pretty much always a bad idea – even if you are a teacher yourself – and so it is very likely that this would have resulted in some very serious consequences. However, I was there and therefore able, after a fashion, to help the assistant head understand the situation and why it was the autistic student was reacting so badly. Happily, they listened and understood, and the original perpetrators were given the detention, and my student was in less trouble, though was still given a reprimand for using violent physical behaviour. But I will never forget the few moments I spent with them while I worked out what had happened. The raw emotion and misery on their face, the absolute frustration with a system that did not work and, in all honesty, probably never could work. I have never seen a 16-year-old look so tired, so worn. It shook me to my core and I realized how huge an issue this was.

The fact is, that if we autistic folk are as intolerant of injustice as I suspect we are, then there are millions of us, every single day, having to make the best of living in a world that is inherently and automatically unjust. We are trapped. There are no superheroes out there to save us, or ensure that justice gets done, and so we put ourselves at great risk by trying to argue the case. Much like for my 16-year-old student, there is always a form of punishment for trying to tackle inequity and unfairness established by those in charge. For him, it was detention or – much worse – expulsion. For others, particularly in countries like the United States, arguing with the wrong person in a position of authority can lead to much more dangerous outcomes. After all, there are reports of autistic people getting shot and killed by police officers fairly regularly. Most don't make it to the British media but occasionally a story will slip through. Sometimes it's because the autistic person didn't follow orders, or behaved in a way the officer didn't expect. Often it is because the autistic person argued back.

Yet still we do it. The hours of airtime and acres of print dedicated to tearing down Greta Thunberg does not seem to have lessened her desire to continue the fight. After all, the approaching climate disaster is, perhaps, the very best example of a clear truth that, for whatever reason, people are able to cast aside and ignore; all the while, autistic folks, for the most part lacking that ability to blithely discard obvious facts, are up in arms and moved to try to improve the situation, our brains seemingly incapable of deluding ourselves that all is well and absolutely incensed by the unfairness and lack of sense on display.

I suppose the Marvel Cinematic Universe came at exactly the right time for me, given how difficult the last five years have been. It's far from the only fictional world that

I have completely invested in, though – there seems to be a propensity for fascination with heroic escapades in my brain that I have always found suitable subjects for. Before the Marvel films captured my attention so profoundly, I would say that my fix for heroes and villains fighting it out in detailed worlds was achieved by the *Star Wars* films, which continue to have a strong hold over me, despite the fact I struggled to enjoy the last couple of films. Followers of my Twitter account will know how partial I am to the 'Prequel' trilogy – those ones released around the turn of the millennium with Ewan McGregor and the irritating frog man – and I can immerse myself into the lore of the Jedi for days on end.

In my experience, *Star Wars* is probably even more popular amongst autistic people than the Marvel films – perhaps because the delineation between good and evil is even more baldly stated, with the completely good Jedi (with a couple of notable exceptions) and the irredeemably evil Sith (again, with at least one vital exception – Darth Vader himself). It means you're always on good, solid ground when it comes to working out who you can trust, which is vital to me as I cannot bear films where the rug is pulled from our feet with some revelation that such and such a character was evil all along (except for Agatha in *WandaVision*, of course: she was great...).

Something about this kind of 'twist', when employed so that there would be few reasons to suspect the character, upsets me at a primeval level, to the point that any enjoyment had up to the moment of the reveal is erased completely from my mind. It's even worse when the character is a friend of the protagonist, as is so often the case, especially in more gritty TV dramas and the like. I suppose this kind of subversion, in that it upends the entire story, is anathema to the kind of order and routine that I find comfort in. It may be boring, but I am much happier watching a movie where the bad guys are clearly bad, or if they do pretend to be good, it's painfully obvious that they are not!

Along with *Star Wars*, I spent a very long time absolutely immersed in the universe of Harry Potter. I knew each book inside out, could easily name every character and the order they died in, was totally obsessed with the wider fictional universe and looked forward eagerly to new instalments. When the final book was released, in 2007, I stayed up all night to read it through – completely incapable of closing the book – as I simply had to find out how the saga ended. However, my fascination of this particular fiction ended extremely abruptly recently, thanks to comments made by their creator J.K. Rowling. Her views on the trans community are something I cannot agree with – for whatever reason they strike me as unreasonable and unjust, and I found this Special Interest evaporated overnight. I couldn't have stopped this if I had wanted to. I have no interest in proselytizing here: these are simply my views, but it is interesting to me how total the ending of my interest with Potter was. It felt rather like I went to sleep a fan, though troubled by her words, but awoke with absolutely no interest whatsoever – something in my brain had clicked the switch off, and I have no desire to try to turn it back on again. I haven't read or watched any content from that franchise since, and even my desperate desire for the huge and intricate LEGO® Hogwarts Castle disappeared into the ether. Clearly these feelings of right and wrong, and this focus on justice and fairness in all things, can be extremely strong in the autistic mind.

To finish the chapter, a word on one final fictional universe that deserves mention, and one that I have loved for many years – *Lord of the Rings*. It is hard to imagine something more stereotypically nerdy and geeky than this enduring story, and it goes without saying that once again, the fandom is full of autistic people who love the detail of the world building and the veracity of the characters who, despite living in a world where they may find themselves rescued from giant spiders by elven warriors, feel very real indeed. I mention it now because, out of all of the books and films I have mentioned in this chapter, it is this that I feel has a protagonist that I can relate to the best.

It is a dangerous business, speculating on whether fictional characters could be diagnosed as neurodivergent in some way, so I do not wish to suggest that Frodo Baggins, much like his uncle before him, is autistic. He's a hobbit: who knows if such creatures even could be. The point is that Frodo is so very relatable for me as an autistic adult. Even before his adventures he is a definite 'black sheep' of the family, haunted by dreams of wandering off away from the Shire. Once it becomes clear what he needs to do, he just does it, almost by default. He is always separate, aloof, different to the other hobbitses that accompany him on his trek to Mordor, and he sees things that others can't see, feels things that others don't feel and ultimately never feels truly part of the world he lives in.

I remember when I finished the novel for the first time, being agog at the ending, as Frodo leaves Middle Earth to journey over the ocean to the 'Undying Lands'. This is a natural result of his ordeal making him feel disconnected from everything around him, and gives the story an extremely bittersweet ending. I recognized myself in that motive. Not because I had carried a haunted ring up a volcano, but because I, along with every other autistic person, knew exactly how it felt to not really belong in the world. Here was a hero – a genuine hero – who was not at home here. Uncomfortable. Odd.

For ultimately that it is how it is for so many of us autistic people, as we fight our battles and attempt to be heroes in our own lives. We wish to change the world, save the world, help the world, despite not really feeling we are part of it. We are at a remove, strangers in a strange land, yet despite that, so many of us try to improve it for everybody. That, I think, is a powerfully good thing, and something that so many autistic people, whether telling the world's leaders to do something about climate change or writing to a research group about problems with their ethics should rightly be proud of.

CHAPTER EIGHT

Nearer My God to Thee

We finally come, rather paradoxically and confusingly, to the beginning, as well as the end. The ship we call, despite over a century of expansive time, so familiarly by its name *Titanic* (I mean, I've never met her...) was one of my very earliest interests and has persisted throughout my life without anything even approaching a 'quiet spot'. LEGO® never did manage such an accolade, though video games in general come pretty close. Even during the dark moments outlined in Chapter Six, this interest endured quietly. The most famous ship the world has ever known has sat in my brain in much the same way as it continues to sit, alone and forlorn, on the deep plains under the rushing North Atlantic Ocean, off the coast of Newfoundland.

I'm not going to waste your time retelling the story of that cold windless night in mid-April 1912. It has been told a thousand times in a thousand different ways, all of which (it feels) I have at some point consumed. Instead, I'm going to focus on what it is about the story of the *Titanic* that especially piques the interest of my autistic brain, and how it reflects so many fascinating aspects of what being autistic is all about. If you wish to read a good account of the sinking, my recommendation will always be *A Night to Remember* by Walter Lord – as far as I can tell it has never been bettered, though its film adaptation comes very close.

I vividly remember lying in my bunk bed on my stomach, in my bedroom in my grandad's house in Coalville. We had been living there maybe a year as we had struggled due to my dad being made redundant in those truly awful years of the early 90s. It must have been 1992 or so because I could hear my dad's music from my parents' room. He must have been writing essays for university (he was a mature student at this point, studying for a degree in English Literature) and was seemingly, as far as my memory serves, listening to a couple of songs from R.E.M.'s new album *Automatic For the People* on endless repeat. The melodies of 'The Sidewinder Sleeps Tonite' and 'Man on the Moon' are branded on this memory extremely strongly, as I lay there reading a book my dad had got for me from the library.

It was the account of the discovery of the wreck of the *Titanic* in 1985, written by its finder, Robert Ballard, and adorned with what were by a long way the most fascinating pictures I had ever seen. It was absolutely filled with diverting, horrifying stills of the wreck and its associated debris field. There were looming artistic representations of what the bow section (for the ship had splintered as it sank) would look like were you able to sufficiently pierce the intense blackness to see it from that distance, drawn so realistically by Ken Marschall that it took me weeks to realize they were not – never could be – photographs.

By far the most morbidly intriguing images were of the debris field that covers the expanse of sea floor between the two halves of the wreck. A whole section of the book was given over to these, dozens of little snaps taken by the robotic 'sled' that had scoured the area looking for indications of the ship.

The first hint of the wreck spotted by Ballard's team was a grainy image of one of the ship's many boilers – huge cylinders adorned with three holes in the lower half of their flat face, portals through which coal would have been endlessly and exhaustingly shovelled by the firemen. The image shows the distinctive pattern of coal holes and the array of rivets that festooned it. It was this that confirmed to Ballard that the wreck had finally been discovered, but it wasn't the most interesting picture taken. Others spoke more to the humanity of the site. Piles of white crockery, still held together, as the wooden cabinet that held them rotted away to nothing. Suitcases and bags, the leather managing to withstand the corrosive processes two miles down. The ceramic, white head of a child's doll – looking at first disturbingly like a skull – found lying on the sediment by the buried bow of the ship. Pairs of shoes, still lying side by side, shadowy reminders that those who died and sank with the ship had vanished in the intervening 73 years.

I absorbed every single one of these grim reminders of mortality, at the young age of nine years old, as R.E.M. played in the background. It seems that some Special Interests are different to the others. Whilst so many of those that I have outlined in this book are joyful, or calming, or exciting, or just fun, this one has always been maudlin and emotional, capable of bringing me to tears, but still magnetic, drawing me in in a way the other fixations never have.

The *Titanic* is by far my most emotional interest and my most powerful.

Autistic people aren't meant to have emotion, of course. If one were to listen to the popular ebb and flow of discussion and media representation, you'd be forced to think that autistic people are robots – emotionless, cold, remorselessly logical, and rigid in interpretation. Autistic people don't cry. They don't laugh. They don't feel sadness, or loss, or pain, or despair. We just trundle on, as emotionally complex as a tricycle.

It sounds so silly saying it out loud like this, but it has to be acknowledged that this is the state of common understanding. If you were to type into Google's search bar 'can autistic people...', and let the autocomplete function perform its magic, you will see the most common questions that the populace of Earth asks its electronic advisor are:

- Can autistic people feel empathy?

- Can autistic people cry?

- Can autistic people laugh?

- Can autistic people feel love?

❖

If you are in any doubt at all, I can assure you that the vast majority of autistic people can do or feel all of these things, and without any issue whatsoever. But the fact anyone has to ask shows how behind the times and backward-facing public perception is. As an autistic person, I am horrified by it – why would someone think that autistic people are incapable of feeling emotion, of laughing, of feeling love? Even if in some specific circumstances this *is* the case, it's hardly such a standard thing as to be at the forefront of everyone's minds. It feels sometimes like we are completely misrepresented and misunderstood by, well, pretty much everyone, and it's a depressing feeling.

My interest in the *Titanic* is extremely emotional. I can make myself cry in an instant if I remind myself of the various stories of heroism, loss and personal tragedy that unfolded on that April night. I have sobbed at the 1997 film by James Cameron more times than I'm willing to admit, and not just at the human losses. Perhaps this is where autism starts to show itself, but I also feel a strong empathy with the ship itself. I may feel tears welling up when the Irish mother is tucking her children into bed for the night as the icy waters swirl, or as Ida and Isidor Strauss clutch each other tightly as the ship sinks, but I also feel myself collapsing into tears when the ship splits in two, or at the shots of it quietly rusting deep beneath the Atlantic. My empathy seems to stretch way beyond the human, and I'm not sure that this is a bad thing at all.

Autistic people can be described as having hyper-empathy – in fact it's a very common topic of discussion in the community. There is definitely a consensus that far from being completely lacking in it, we tend to have an overabundance of empathy that can cause us considerable difficulties. The issue has many facets. For example, it makes us emotional sponges. Let's imagine an autistic person blunders innocently into a room, their emotions completely neutral, but the room is occupied by a couple of people engaged in an argument, with bitterness and unhappiness whipped between the two. It seems that a large number of autistic folks would feel that emotion hanging in the air immediately, and not only that, but they would also begin to feel it within themselves too. I have experienced this so many times, finding myself unwillingly taking on other people's emotions when in proximity to them, usually to my detriment. When I was young, I would be able to tell immediately if my parents were in the middle of a fight, even if they attempted to hide it. Similarly, I pick up on the prevailing emotion of a classroom (as a teacher) – if a class is all wound up by some dreadful act or gossip, then I can't fail to feel it on the air.

This would be veering into usefulness if there was anything I could do with this inferred information, but all too often I'm at a loss to specifically identify the emotion I'm picking up on, let alone find a way to remedy it. I absorb it all like a sponge and, like a sponge, just sit there, until someone comes along to wring me out and help me get back to normal. This is why the stereotype of alien, robotic autistic people is so bewildering to us, as it's so extraordinarily wrong. I suppose it must be based on something, of course, and so I have concluded it is probably a result of misinterpreting how we *handle* emotion, and perhaps how we display it on our own selves.

The thing is, even if we are feeling a thick myriad of emotions, it's likely that the people around us will struggle to notice. There are a few good reasons for this. First, as I have touched upon, we struggle to know how to use emotion. We may feel empathy extremely strongly, but we may not show it in the way neurotypical people do. If I'm sitting with a sad person, I will know something is wrong, but I won't immediately go over to hug them. It simply wouldn't occur to me, and even if it did, I would second guess their reaction into oblivion, terrifying myself that comforting them might be misunderstood. By the time I had steeled myself to approach them, they'd probably have cheered up and gone. To be honest it would likely be the next day.

Second, we are often very bad at identifying exactly what our emotions are at any time. This is called alexithymia and is very common amongst autistic folks. We feel the emotions, but we're damned if we could name them or point to them on one of those charts of cartoon faces that autistic kids are given. As such, we absorb it all but may well be stumped beyond that. Perhaps we can tell it's a generally negative set of emotions that we've taken on board, but there's less chance of breaking it down more specifically than that. Thus, we don't reliably react appropriately to emotional situations – a source of comedic gold for sitcom writers the world over.

Third, we are likely to have what is called 'flat affect'. This is where an autistic person's emotions are not transmitted properly to their face – the result being a kind of constant 'poker face'. It is possible, for example, for an autistic child to receive an amazing Christmas gift – just what they had always wanted – and be absolutely ecstatic, only for their mum to pipe up, 'Cheer up, love!' because their face isn't displaying their emotion. So many huge holiday arguments stem from this particular issue, as I can personally attest. It is not quite the same thing as the famous 'resting bitch face', which is something that anyone in the population can have, but it is similar in terms of effect. I personally find joy and contentment hard to express, but I haven't yet worked out whether this is genuine flat affect or just my overactive brain overthinking and worrying that whatever expression I am making looks false or fake in some way.

Of course this, out of all of these factors, can be the most unsettling for onlookers, and I would hazard that it is the primary driver behind the myth of us lacking emotion. But of course, the emotion is there, flailing around behind our inscrutable faces. So even if we manage to figure out what emotion is going on, and somehow have the wherewithal to act appropriately to help the poor soul suffering, we may do so with a complete lack of obvious emotion on our own faces. Talk about a perfect storm.

With all of this going on, I suppose it isn't too much of a surprise that neurotypicals have misunderstood what's going on 'under the bonnet', as it were. Interestingly, though, one outflow of our emotional inner life is reasonably well known outside of the autistic community: our collective love of animals and, by extension, our love of objects, things, and items. These are different of course: I'm not about to start claiming your little pet hamster is simply an 'item', as that would be wrong. But I believe our overriding love for living things *other than humans*, and our love of our favourite objects, stems from the same source – the overactive empathy I mentioned earlier, whereby we feel true sympathy for things that aren't people.

Most autistic people have an affinity for nature, and this isn't the place for me to dive too deeply into this – best to settle down and read some of Dara McAnulty's writing to really get a grasp of this – yet it deserves to be touched upon. Often, the love of nature will revolve around a concern for it – a worry, for example, that the dog you saw outside a shop has been abandoned by its owner, or a fear that the cat you saw hiding under a van is going to bolt into the road and be hit by a car. Autistic children often need a lot of support with managing these strong, fearful emotions as their imaginations dart around all of the awful, saddening consequences that might occur should an animal find themselves in danger.

I myself cannot see a dog tied up to railings by its lead, howling and crying for its owner (who, let's face it, has probably been AWOL for all of 30 seconds and has just nipped into Waitrose to buy a sandwich) without feeling absolutely devastated that the poor thing is trapped in some personal dystopia, its owner dead somewhere, its lead tight around its neck, the chance of a happy life forever receding into the distance. I just can't help it – my mind zooms to these questionable destinations on autopilot. Typically, I will have to hang around, looking like a dishevelled loiterer (we autistic folk can look quite dishevelled sometimes – you try looking dapper when the world is out to get you all the time), until the friendly and clearly deeply compassionate owner emerges from the shop, feeds the little pup a piece of the sandwich they've bought for themselves and they merrily skip away together to their next exciting adventure. I stare after them, tears drying around my eyes, and continue on inevitably to the next tied-up dog.

But what fed my love and compassion for the *story* of what happened to the *Titanic* was my love and compassion for the boat itself. It is highly personified in my mind – pretty much a character in its own right. I know its every curve and rivet, and can't help but see a 'face', of sorts, in the forward-facing open decks of its superstructure. Go and find any illustration of the ship and look at the forward part of the superstructure – can you see the face? Because I sure as hell do. Pareidolia is a fascinating thing.

As far as my brain is concerned, the ship was *born* in Belfast, started work and then died in a terrible work-related accident. For whatever reason, my mind works hard to maintain the idea that the boat requires empathy and didn't deserve what happened to it. Not only that, but I feel bad for it too – a kind of vicarious pity that it should have had to deal with such things. If I discover anyone trying to pin the blame for the accident on the ship itself, I feel highly offended on the boat's behalf – no, it wasn't made of sub-standard iron, and no, it wasn't poorly designed. It was, for its time, excellently well built: it was the nature of the accident, all of the elements synchronizing at that one fatal moment, that sealed the ship's, and all her passengers', fates. Just to illustrate this, here are the many dismal coinciding events that conspired to cause the wreck:

- Missing binoculars, locked in a case whose key was held by a senior officer (David Blair) who was reshuffled off the crew in Southampton, meant the lookouts had no means of identifying distant objects. Unlikely to have helped, but still...

- Absolute flat calm – there was no wind at all, hence no waves lapping at the base of the iceberg, which would have made it much more noticeable.

- Moonless night – starlight alone isn't great to travel by...

- The manoeuvre around the iceberg could have worked, but instead (incredibly unfortunately) punched holes between plates over one too many watertight compartments.

- This holing of one extra of these compartments sealed its fate as it tipped the scales, literally. Water would now fill and then overtop each bulkhead, one after the other. Not many ships sink in this way.

- The absolute lack of any nearby shipping – pretty unusual for this busy route – and the fact that the *Californian*, which was in range, was asleep for the night.

⁜

The most robustly built ship on Earth would struggle to overcome such heavily weighted-against conditions.

I told myself I would not bore you with such extraneous detail about the sinking, but as you may have guessed, just the idea of someone thinking ill of my beloved boat forced me to enter Defensive Mode. It just feels so deeply *unreasonable* to go after one of the victims of the catastrophe, for that is what the ship is, in my mind.

It goes way beyond the *Titanic*, though. My ability to feel empathy for inanimate objects seems to know no bounds, and it can be curiously troublesome. For a start, it can be a catalyst towards the development of a hoarding mentality. After all, how can anything be thrown away if you feel pity for stuff you put in the bin? I am fairly sure that if it weren't for the influence of ADHD, constantly forcing me to renew and refresh my surroundings, I would be living amongst a lifetime's detritus – only, of course, I wouldn't view it that way, as I would be truly attached to every item.

As it is, my object empathy tends to skew in a few directions. One is more understandable and is based primarily on association. So, for example, I may see a discarded child's shoe or, worse, soft toy on the pavement in the rain. I will feel both the loss for the child – that gnawing sense of pain that the poor thing won't see its beloved bear again – but also the opposite: the (imagined) sadness of the bear itself, left forlorn and alone on a cold bit of asphalt. It's pathetic fallacy on a grand scale. I will feel a very real sense of abandonment and sorrow that will be strong enough to affect the rest of my day if I let it. The link between the child and the toy is the key in this example.

The other way my object empathy can materialize is a bit stranger, but appears to be pretty common amongst autistic people. This is where we view the object as an independent, sentient being (or at least we seem to – there's no direct delusion at work here, and I am always aware of the oddness of the situation) and treat it as such. So, for example, we may wish to be fair with our kitchen utensils, ensuring every piece gets a 'run out' from time to time, for fear of the big ladle getting bored or the fish slice feeling abandoned. It is behind the feeling of togetherness we may have with a particular item of clothing that we feel great affinity with – perhaps our shoes or a special sweater. It might even be directed at an object someone else is unhappy with: a number of times I have seen someone be rough with a door handle, say, and felt the need to protect it and tell the person to back off. A key memory of mine that illustrates this well happened when I was around ten years old. The early 90s saw a re-release of the classic kid's TV show *Thunderbirds*, and for a while I was absolutely hooked. The combination of miniatures, explosions and drama was enough to make me utterly besotted. As such, I needed to fill my life with *Thunderbirds* paraphernalia, which I did with gusto and surprising speed. I had all the little metal models of the ships (if you're not familiar with the show, it was a puppet-based drama series where a group of men used rocket ships and submarines of various types to rescue folk – well, other puppets – from disaster and chaos) and I collected the excellent weekly magazine.

My absolute favourite story featured a huge, many-legged machine that was designed to traverse difficult terrain, which fell into a huge pit. As the temperature in the pit rose (for reasons I cannot recall), the peril grew, with the erstwhile Thunderbird crews struggling to work out how to rescue the poor overheated puppets on board before they presumably set alight. And this week that episode was the focus of the magazine! I was delighted and sat at my dining table with all my *Thunderbirds* stuff spread out, eagerly absorbing the extra information the magazine fed me.

My mother was in a bad mood. To be completely fair to her, she had every reason to be – lack of sleep, thanks to my two-year-old sister's peculiar sleeping habits (she refused to sleep upstairs) and us living in a cramped three-bed house with my grandad made for a pretty difficult set of circumstances – but nevertheless she was not happy to see my magazines and toys scattered across the table. In her annoyance she muttered, 'Get this shit off the table,' and I immediately broke down. Not because I had been told off – I hadn't really, after all – but because I felt it was so unreasonable and horrible to refer to all this brilliant stuff as 'shit'. I took it extremely personally on behalf of my inanimate magazines and toys, and it is testament to how big a deal it was that I remember it so very clearly to this day, nearly 30 years later. I would bet money on my poor mum not recalling the event at all: after all, why should she? But it looms large in my memory of the time, and I felt desperately sorry for my *Thunderbirds* magazines for a very long time afterwards.

So, it is a very interesting trait of autism that we should feel this link and connection to all things, whether human, animal or mineral. As for other objects that faced disaster, I have very similar feelings of sadness and pity for the *Challenger* and *Columbia* space shuttles, the *Lusitania*, the *Costa Concordia* and the World Trade Center, to name but a few.

❖

My interest in the *Titanic* has never faltered. It remains as strong now as it was back in the early 90s, and I continue to find new and interesting avenues to explore my interest through. As a child it was all about model-making. I had a cardboard cut-out model of the ship in the process of sinking – the famous moment where its stern is at a 45° angle high out of the water – and I poured an inordinate amount of time into constructing a very large multicolour LEGO® *Titanic* out of all of my spare pieces. It even had a weakened area two thirds along where, with a bit of applied force, the model would snap in two. I *was* a rather morbid child.

Later in life, I was more concerned with the clinical details of the sinking, reading *A Night to Remember* many times and survivors' accounts of the wreck. When *Minecraft®* crashed into my world, one of the first things I did was build a life-size model of the whole ship, based on the original blueprints, that allows me to explore the boat at my leisure. It is moored off the coast of the vast world I discussed in Chapter Six, and it may be one of my very favourite creations in that game. Walking the decks and bridge and grand staircases of my model is as close as I'm likely to get to experiencing the ship itself.

This model ship had an extra purpose – or at least I told myself it did, in order to justify the time and effort. In late 2012 I managed to get onto a famous BBC quiz show: *Mastermind*. I had applied as a joke, mostly – just to see what would happen – and was very surprised when they rang me back, just as I was stressed boarding a busy train to London. Being unrelentingly autistic, I don't deal very well with unexpected phone calls and will usually leave them to voicemail, but I didn't this time. Instead, as I fought to get to my seat through the seemingly endless throngs, I was being interviewed by a faceless, nameless voice. This interview consisted of being asked a rapid flurry of general knowledge questions. It ended just as I finally sat down, bewildered and exhausted.

Typically, I assumed I couldn't possibly have done very well, and thought that would be the end of it. But no. Somehow, I had impressed enough through my muttered swear words and rushed answers for a second interview, this time in person at the BBC's Bristol studios. As with all things in my life (and I include the opportunity to write this book in this), I just ran with it without giving it too much thought and turned up at the studios more or less by autopilot (if I reflect back on life this feeling of just passively following the currents of life is definitely a recurring theme, and one I can't decide whether to chalk up to autism or ADHD... perhaps it's a bit of both). This session I remember a little better than the train incident – sitting in a bland office room across from a few producers (all of whom were so much younger than me – the media business is such a youthful one) who flung more and more general knowledge questions at me, over and over, almost like they were trying to break me.

I suppose in some ways they were – after all, it's in their interests to ensure anyone who ends up in the famous black leather chair and its associated blinding spotlight is going to handle the pressure and not immediately melt into a pool of fear. But I like trivia and being asked questions is second nature to me as a teacher, so I think I glided through that with relative ease. It's surprisingly autism-friendly: no real small talk or expectation of social chatter – just a very straightforward and structured set of tasks. That was that: I was going to be on the show.

The thing is, Mastermind has a gimmick at its heart that makes it particularly good for autistic folks (who I suspect make up a significant proportion of its participants). When you apply, you must choose a 'specialist subject' – basically a topic that you know so much about, that you've immersed yourself in for so long, that you feel confident you can answer 25 or so questions on the topic under intense pressure. Because it's possible you may appear in three episodes (heats, semis and the final), you need to add two further topics that would be used in those happy circumstances. That's three subjects you need to be essentially 'expert' in: it's the autistic person's dream. For my last two I did struggle – many of my interests don't lend themselves to trivia, and those that do are pretty inappropriate (it will be a cold day in hell before the BBC let someone answer questions on Warhammer). In the end I went with *Alice's Adventures in Wonderland*, for reasons I honestly don't recall, and, fittingly, the band R.E.M., including their history, discography and biographies. Sadly, these never came into play, as I didn't reach the semis, but my first choice still served me well. Of course, I chose the *Titanic*.

This wouldn't be the first time that the *Titanic* had proved useful in a trivia game. When I was around 18, one of the regular social events I would frequent was the weekly quiz down at a local pub, the White Horse. It is a stereotypical English pub, a thatched building squatting cosily by the main town bridge over the River Welland in Spalding town centre, all whitewashed walls and little nooks and crannies to sit happily in and enjoy the suspiciously cheap drinks. The quiz was mostly populated by middle-aged folk and pensioners – it was that kind of establishment – but this didn't faze me or my friends at all: it was a safe space, a place to drink beer without being prey to the more socially adept men that we shared our sixth form common room with. The fact that this pleasant, cheap haven came with a quiz attached was simply a bonus.

I have never had a huge issue with socializing in the standard way, so long as alcohol is involved somewhere. It feels to me – and I speak as someone who these days barely touches a drop thanks to how it interferes with my medications – that a pint or two of beer has the effect of erasing some of the social anxiety that I always feel. I relax a little, feel more confident in chatting, and become (I have been told) funnier as a result. The use of alcohol as a means to an end for autistic people could fill a book by itself, so I shall leave it at that, but for me it was a lubricant that didn't just help social interaction: it *enabled* it completely.

And so it was that I was feeling a little fuzzy after

perhaps three pints of their best ale when the quiz was drawing to a close. We had performed badly in the main section, but the bonus 'Jackpot' moment was approaching, carrying its prize of £20. Traditionally these had been very difficult questions, with answers that tended to be numerical and impossible to say with precision. Teams would usually win by giving the best guess. Not this week. The question rang out over the pub's speakers: 'How many lifeboats did the *Titanic* have?'

I still feel good about that moment now, 20 years later (the answer is 20, by the way – 14 standard boats, two 'cutters' and four 'collapsibles').

Back to the BBC studios in Manchester: I remember some of the questions I was asked by famous grouch John Humphreys, sitting in the big black (and surprisingly roomy and comfortable) chair – but mostly they're the ones I got wrong. How typical is it of my general mindset to fixate on my failures even as I did pretty well? I scored 27 points, which honestly isn't too bad, but it wasn't enough to beat my opponent's almost supernaturally good 33. But my knowledge of the *Titanic*, honed and developed over the years since listening to 'Man on the Moon' on my bed whilst reading about this lost, great ship, was there. I had put one of my Special Interests to use.

Yet I'm still far prouder of winning the pub quiz.

⚜

I am 38 now, and *Mastermind* was nine years ago. It feels like another lifetime, and that's because it was. I didn't know anything about autism back then, much less that I was autistic myself, and at 29 years of age was still fairly immature and naive about most things. I'm older now, wiser and more cynical – attuned to the unpleasant unfairness of the world and far more knowledgeable about my own brain and its take on reality.

However, age and autism are two subjects that rarely merge. The durable perception of autism being a childhood condition is so pervasive that many older autistic people – we call ourselves the 'elders' of the community – feel absolutely abandoned by society at large, as once we grew older, we vanished into nothingness. There is no research into how the aging process interacts with autism. Nothing at all, for example, on the way that menopause might cause people's autistic traits to amplify or whatever – quite an enormous problem when you consider how the hormonal rollercoaster of puberty is well researched in comparison. We are all of us growing older and older, day by day, with absolutely no idea what we are heading for.

I worry most about how it will be for autistic people who have to enter non-specialist residential care – just your ordinary old people's homes. At the other end of a lifetime, school can be extremely hostile to autistic children unless the teachers and support staff are well educated and trained on how autism manifests in the various individuals in their care, but at least there is a sustained effort to make this the case. Schools have SENCOs, the Special Educational Needs officers whose job is to ensure that the full range of children get the support they need.

Autistic training is at least ostensibly in place in schools, and initial teacher training (ITT) has a focus on it too.

Does the elderly care sector have these safeguards in place? The answer is a predictable 'no'. Apart from a couple of outliers, there is little explicit awareness or understanding of autism amongst care home staff, least of all specific understanding of how autism intersects with age. It simply isn't there. So, there will be – unproven but I would go so far as to stake my reputation on it – thousands of autistic elderly people in care homes across the UK (and, of course, huge numbers more overseas) who are almost certainly undiagnosed and who receive no specific support suitable for their needs at all.

I posted a poll on Twitter just yesterday, where I asked my followers how they felt about growing old as autistic people. Admittedly, not the most scientific approach, but given the lack of anything else on the subject is surely worth considering. I got just over 1500 responses and a huge 76 per cent of autistic respondents over the age of 35 were either 'concerned' by the prospect of aging, or flat-out 'terrified'. The written replies to the polling tweet illuminated a vast array of worries, from financial concerns to worries about an increasing frequency of meltdowns and burnouts. Many were scared of loneliness, which I think is a fairly standard concern of aging, but amongst those a common refrain was a worry of being lonely and therefore having no specific autistic support network, the like of which now they have thanks, mostly, to the Internet.

The sad truth is that none of us have much of an idea what to expect. The few autistic elders that do exist in the community – and by that, I mean those over around 60 years of age – are happy to share their experiences (many of which are quite frightening) but are obviously a very limited pool of data to draw from. As we age, we enter a dark, empty, unmapped space that is extremely threatening in its mystery. Here be dragons.

For myself, there are patterns that have begun to emerge that give clues as to what might be coming. Since the burnout I described in Chapter Six, I have noticed I am much quicker to reach a meltdown state than I used to be. In my twenties, meltdowns were relatively rare – perhaps a handful a year; now, in my late thirties, I have several a month, and sometimes more. If this progresses as I expect it to, then perhaps I can expect to have to deal with very regular meltdowns, perhaps two or more a week. I'm not sure I have the capacity to deal with how exhausting that would be.

I have also noticed that my anxiety has got more profound, rather than less. Many people talk about how age enables a person to relax more, be more confident in themselves and care less about how others view them, but I am finding it to be the opposite. I am pretty much constantly wracked by anxiety, most of it originating in some autistic trait or another, and find it almost impossible to relax or stay truly calm. If I do manage to find an oasis of peace, it invariably lasts for less than ten minutes before my brain seems to rebel and demand that I return to worrying about things. I am, as you would imagine, extremely worried about this getting worse.

Finally, the impact on executive function. As I have

briefly mentioned before, executive function is a set of jobs the brain manages, all related to motivation, planning, prioritizing, scheduling and completing. For most autistic people, and pretty much all ADHD folks, there is significant dysfunction here: that part of our brains simply doesn't work very well. As such, many autistic people are incredibly disorganized, to a level neurotypical people often find hard to believe, and this can have an enormously detrimental effect on our lives. The problem is, for me at least, the issue seems to be getting worse and worse. Don't get me wrong: I have never been organized, as any of my teachers, employers or colleagues would tell you (grumpily and with an air of extreme irritation), but these last few years, since turning 35 or so, I am finding myself more and more incapable of keeping everything together and proper.

After all, adulthood is simply an exponential increase to the complexity of life, and I feel that I am not equal to it. The number of different pieces of administration I have to keep tabs on seems to grow year by year, with deadlines, reminders, appointments all jostling around in a chaotic cloud in my head. I try my best to wrestle it under control – I use electronic and physical calendars and planners and the like, but the problem is that none of these things work if you don't remember to check them, and I forget to all the time. It is honestly a wonder that this book has got this far, and even then, I can't help feeling it's likely that you, the reader, will turn a page only to find it stops in mid-sentence.

How this will be in ten years or so, I simply cannot

imagine. I hope, probably naively, that I will 'snap out of it', and perhaps enjoy better mental health which will then trigger better executive function. But deep down I am very aware of how unlikely this is. I, like every autistic person there is, will have to accept that growing old autistic is inevitably going to bring a huge range of difficulties to handle and try to overcome.

My love of the *Titanic* endures, though. Like every interest in this book, it may have occasionally dropped out of focus, but ultimately it remains and presumably always will do. There are hundreds of more temporary interests that I could have populated this book with, by the way – most lasting between a month to a year or so – and other long-term interests that I avoided mentioning, mostly because I didn't quite know what to say about them (say hello, trains and *Thomas the Tank Engine*!). The *Titanic*, though, will forever have a special place in my pantheon of obsessions, thanks mostly to my experience of being on the television as a result of it, and the emotional hold it has over me. At the time of writing, the LEGO® company have revealed their latest, greatest huge set: a 9000-piece behemoth. It is, of course, a fully detailed and exquisitely beautiful model of the *Titanic*. And so, my two most enduring interests collide. Sadly, at a price point of nearly £600, it is likely to be forever out of reach. I couldn't let it pass without comment though, as the coincidence alone of it finally happening – an official LEGO® *Titanic* set! – just as I was editing my chapters on those two very subjects was too fascinating to ignore.

For now, I will be content with the memory of the ship I built out of multicoloured bricks, all those years ago – after all, the most wonderful thing about these autistic interests is how they inspire us, energize us and give us the motivation to keep on going.

Epilogue

I wrote this book, first and foremost, because I wanted to finally say everything I have ever needed to about all of these things that I hold so extremely dear to myself. In doing so, I feel that I have finally managed to clear some space in my head, like a person who never throws anything away finally getting around to at least organizing their vast collection of stuff. A few paths have now been carved through the vast amount of all of this that I carry around in my head, and as such it is easier to look through, to explore and to find the things I need.

I truly hope that sharing all of this proved to be interesting, and that perhaps you have even managed to find some curiosity for topics and subjects that you previously had absolutely no interest in – that would be fantastic. Similarly, I hope it has enabled you to understand the vital importance Special Interests and Hyperfixations have in the lives of autistic people like myself. They keep us going, feed and nurture us and help us maintain our mood and capacity for stress, but they also delight us, fill our world with beauty and fascination: they are everything, at least to me.

The world is still not safe for autistic people, much like

it remains hostile to nearly all minorities. To be autistic in this world is to live a confusing, frightening and, most of all, extremely stressful life. From those first experiences in nursery school to the slog of working life, autistic people fight to be understood and, even more importantly, accepted. It's hard work. I spend the majority of my time writing not about my favourite, fun things that I enjoy, but instead the stresses and strains of being autistic, the difficulties we have with communication, social interaction, sensory oversensitivity. We are disabled, after all – autism is very much a disability and a pretty serious one at times, but much of the disability is wrought by a world around us that is rigid and cold, unwilling to adjust itself to help meet our needs.

Perhaps after reading this book, you will think more about this, and do more to try to help the neurodivergent people in your lives to enjoy a safer, calmer world. Don't make this the only book on autism you read, and don't make me the only person writing about autism that you'll take notice of! There is a large community of autistic people online, just itching to tell you everything they know about what it is to grow up and live autistic. Get on Twitter, Facebook, Instagram and TikTok and follow them, read their words and watch their videos.

It is possible that autistic people will be accepted by a more inclusive, more accepting society, but it doesn't happen by magic. It takes work. There's an awful lot of prejudice out there, and poorly constructed opinions about what autistic people need and what we 'deserve', in employment, education, health, justice and beyond.

It often feels like the outlook is pretty bleak, but there are signs of improvement as adult autistic people speak up and try to effect change.

So, meet us halfway and maybe that inclusive, kind world can be realized.